In Praise of Vikki Claflin

"**Vikki Claflin has a Xena,** Warrior Princess-like approach to life, wielding her pen and disarming challenges through humor. I find Vikki both funny and courageous, and that just happens to be my favorite combination."

~Donna Highfill, Blogger, *Damenation*

"**Vikki has written a gem.** She masterfully presents her Parkinson's with humor, making the reader quickly realize that Vikki is an amazing soul. This is a light and quick read that will make you feel good. Anyone who can make me laugh out loud and feel good when reading about a chronic disease is an author I will return to time and time again."

~Andrea Peskind Katz, Blogger, *Great Thoughts*

"**Upon first reading one of Vikki's posts,** I suggested she include a reader warning that said, "Do Not Drink and Read!" As there was no such warning, I attempted to drink a morning cup of coffee while reading a post she'd written, and ended up laughing so hard I spewed coffee all over myself and my computer. Whether she's writing about marriage, or aging gracefully, or living with Parkinson's, anything written by Vikki Claflin is sure to make you laugh. She's just that good."

~Marcia Shaw Wyatt, Blogger, *Blogitudes*

"**It's not easy to write about illness** and make it entertaining and funny, but author Vikki Claflin does it with a deft touch and true voice. Whether you have Parkinson's or not, you'll enjoy every word of Vikki's writing. She takes you into her life and makes you feel right at home, while poking fun at everything—especially herself."

~Sharon Greenthal, Managing Partner and Editor-in-Chief, *Midlife Boulevard*

"**Having a father with not only a great sense of humor,** but Parkinson's as well, taught me one great lesson: You've got to keep laughing through a day of tremors. There is no one—I mean no one—that makes me laugh more than Vikki Claflin. If laughter is the best medicine, you'll get a daily dose from Vikki. This book is guaranteed to put a smile on your face, whether you or someone you love suffers from Parkinson's."

~Ronna Benjamin, Managing Editor/Partner, *Better After 50*

"**Vikki approaches living with a chronic illness** with levity and enviable grace. She proves the old adage, 'Laughter is the best medicine,' to be true. It doesn't take a Parkinson's diagnosis to be able to relate, and most importantly, laugh along with her."

~Michelle Stephens, Blogger, *Juicebox Confession*

"**Vikki Claflin will have you smiling** from page one of *Shake, Rattle, and Roll With It.* I've seen Parkinson's up close and personal. I assure you this writer uses a deft hand to describe the daily struggles with this disease — but never as a pity party! This book is for everyone who believes in the power of humor and the human spirit."

~Kimberly "Kimba" Dalferes,
Author, *I Was In Love With a Short Man Once*

"**Before I launched my own blog,** I admired fantastically funny women bloggers from the cheap seats. One writer who I truly identified with was Vikki Claflin of Laugh Lines. Vikki's positive and funny (and positively funny) outlook on life is completely refreshing. While her Parkinson's is different from my multiple sclerosis, we share the same mantra—It's okay to laugh."

~Leigh-Mary Hoffman, Blogger, *Happily Ever Laughter*

"**I recently stumbled upon Vikki's blog** and fell in love with her writing. No matter what kind of day I'm having, Vikki's humorous take on life—written as only she can write it –lifts my spirits and makes me laugh."

~Lynne Cobb, Professional Writer, Blogger, *Lynne Cobb*

"**Infectious.** It's the best word I can use to describe Vikki and her writing. I find myself smiling and laughing, nodding and giggling. She makes everything accessible – whether she's talking about marriage, fashion faux pas, or life with Parkinson's, Vikki makes me feel like I'm sitting with one of my besties, having a laugh about it all. Her fresh, lighthearted take on everyday life feeds my spirit and makes me smile."

~Jennifer Hicks, Blogger, *Real Life Parenting*

"**For the longest time,** I didn't even know that Vikki had Parkinson's. That's because her blog is one of the funniest, most cheerful, positive places to be! Any kind of 'poor me' dialogues are not allowed, and we're free to chortle with her as she takes us through her every day! This book is a must-read for anyone seeking positivity in their life."

~Roshni AaMom, Blogger, *American Indian Mom*

"**I never thought I'd laugh out loud** reading about someone living with Parkinson's disease. As the parent of a child with a serious illness, I am inspired by Vikki's humor, and strive to bring the same comic relief into my family's life."

~Emily Cappo, Blogger, *Oh Boy Mom*

"**Vikki writes about life** with disease the same way she writes about everything else in her life: lightly, cheerfully and wisely. I remember reading Vikki's 'coming out' post, where she first publicly discussed life with her Parkinson's disease. As a writer who aims to instill joy in the hearts of her readers, I know this wasn't an easy post for Vikki to write, yet she managed to do it and stay true to her "Vikkiness"—graceful, real and freaking funny!"

~Katia Bishop, Blogger, *I Am the Milk*

Shake,
Rattle &
Roll With It

Living & Laughing
with Parkinson's

VIKKI CLAFLIN

Illustrations by Meghan Moylan

Mill Park Publishing
www.MillParkPublishing.com

SECOND EDITION, SEPTEMBER 2016

Published in the United States by Mill Park Publishing 2016

Library of Congress has cataloged this edition as follows:
Claflin, Vikki 1956, September 11 - Shake, Rattle and Roll With It: Living and Laughing with Parkinson's/by Vikki Claflin – 1st U.S. ed.

ISBN: 978-0-9975-8718-0

Book cover by Michele Fairbanks, Fresh Design
Illustrations by Meghan Moylan
Edited by Cathryn Castle

Dedicated to anyone living with, or who loves someone living with, a chronic disease. Someday they will find a cure. Until then, we must laugh.

And to Hubs, who's never read my blog, so will probably never see this, but who taught me the value of a good belly laugh (and a great Cabernet).

I love you.

Acknowledgments

Cathryn Castle, my writing coach/editor and friend, with a beautiful and generous spirit. You helped me create a dream, and then showed me how to go get it. You may not be able to see your angel wings, but they've always been there.

Meghan Moylan, my fabulous illustrator. Your talent and willingness to work with a crazy writer whom you've never actually met made the process even more fun. This book is better because of you.

My blogger buddies on Facebook, especially from The Women of Midlife, Bloppy Bloggers, and Better After 50 for your enthusiastic support and encouragement to jump into the deep end of the writing pool and publish my book, even when I was unsure if it would ever be read by anyone other than my mother and my Chihuahua. YOU ROCK.

My readers. Without you, this book would not exist. Your laughter and responses to my posts carried me through the difficult patches and never let me quit. "You made me laugh out loud" is the greatest compliment you can give a humor writer. Thank you.

Preface

By Cathryn Castle

When I first met Vikki, she was poised and polished, smiling at me from behind the cosmetics counter at a posh boutique. I'm the kind of woman who's more at home in a hardware store than the sophisticated setting of a "girlie stuff" store, but Vikki's warmth and bright smile made me feel at ease amongst the lip gloss and mascara displays. I'm still not sure whether the bright smile was because she's a naturally friendly person or because she was thrilled at the site of a woman who clearly needed a "beauty intervention." Maybe it was both.

Anyway, she sat me down in front of a tray of cosmetics and quickly went to work. While she primed my skin, concealed my dark spots, defined my cheekbones and truly worked a makeup miracle on me, we chatted.

"What do you do?" Vikki asked.

"I'm a journalist. I work as a magazine editor and book publisher," I replied.

"Oooohhh, I'm a writer. A humor writer," she said.

We talked some more, and while she applied foundation, mascara, gloss and stuff, we agreed that we'd love to meet again and talk about our mutual love of writing. I left the boutique with a bag full of assorted cosmetics — and a budding friendship.

We met regularly for drinks and dished happily over books and blogging. When Vikki would share her most recent blog posts with me, I'd marvel at how she could turn even the darkest situation into something downright hilarious. We laughed. A lot. Sometimes Vikki's Parkinson's tremor was apparent. Sometimes not. But she never once mentioned it. Ever.

One Saturday afternoon, several months later, we met for lunch to celebrate Vikki's recent inclusion in an anthology of humor bloggers.

She presented me with a copy of the book, beaming with pride on being published. We toasted her success with margaritas. I looked over at her and asked, "So when will you write about your Parkinson's?" And that's when Vikki spewed margarita out of her nose.

"You knew?" she whispered.

"Well, yes. It is Parkinson's, isn't it?"

"Yes."

I felt embarrassed and a little bit ashamed for saying it out loud. I apologized. And then I said, "Vikki, your Parkinson's is part of your story. An important part. It's real. And it's the truth. How would it be if you wrote about it?"

The following Monday, Vikki, in her own words, "came out" on her blog.

She wrote about the often hilarious and sometimes poignant side of living with Parkinson's disease. (Both Michael J. Fox and the Barrow Institute/ Muhammad Ali Foundation shared her post on Twitter.) And the rest, as they say, is history. She kept writing and writing about it, until a book came to life.

I am shaking, rattling and rolling with pride over how brave, and beautiful, and raw, and honest – and *funny* – my friend Vikki's writing is.

And that she's sharing her story here.

Table of Contents

Part 1
On Shaky Ground (The Early Years)

Part 2
Finding the Funny

Table of Contents

Part 3
It Takes a Village

Table of Contents

Part 1

On Shaky Ground
(The Early Years)

"I can be changed
by what happens to me,
but I refuse
to be reduced by it."

~Maya Angelou

Today I Came Out on My Blog.
(No, It's Not What You Think)

My mother used to call it the "elephant in the room."
It's that one thing everybody *knows*, but nobody wants to mention at any group gathering. Uncle Buck's not at the family Christmas dinner because he ran off with little Suzie's kindergarten teacher, but nobody asks about his empty seat at the table. Bob got fired last week, and now everybody at the office summer bbq pretends they never knew anyone named Bob. Sally had breast cancer last year and still has hair the length of a Chihuahua, but no one at her reunion knows if it's okay to ask how she's doing.

We have an elephant at our house. It's called Parkinson's. I was diagnosed a few years ago, after two years of left-hand tremors which I steadfastly ignored. The fact that my mother has it and I was extremely familiar with the signs demonstrates the rather remarkable ability of humans to deny what they don't want to address. I was a pro. In fact, six years later, this is the first time I've admitted *in writing* to having this intensely private, albeit physically obvious condition.

When I could no longer hide the tremors (and Hubs was threatening to throw me over his shoulder and drag me to the doctor, kicking and screaming "There's nothing WRONG with me!" the entire time), I went to a neurologist, who confirmed what Hubs and I already knew. Yep. I had Parkinson's. Well, crap.

For several days, we sat shell-shocked, trying to figure out how much our life would change, and it was months before I told *anyone*. I didn't want to be *that girl*. "You know that woman that works at the boutique downtown?

She has *Parkinson's*."

"That cool yellow Mercedes you see around town?

The woman who drives it has *Parkinson's*." Suddenly it's like your entire life's accomplishments vaporize into a single hushed word. My response to questions about my tremor was always, "I have a pinched nerve."

But as the years went by, my innate irreverence and political incorrectness grew stronger than my fears and I learned to laugh at the impact this disease made on the daily activities of my life.

A couple of months ago, I bought a stupidly expensive smartphone that supposedly takes high-def, fabulous photos. How would I know? My hand shakes so bad when I hold my arm up above boob-level, that, unless the shutter speed is defaulted to "Olympic Sprinter," you're going to be *seriously* out of focus or without a head.

The good news is that if you need a garden or yard seeded, I'm your girl.

My arm is permanently set to "sprinkle lightly," and I can fertilize an acre of lawn faster than Hub's rolling seed sprayer. I'm thinking of hiring out for this one.

I've cut and colored my own hair for years (It's 1/2" long and I'm too cheap to pay for a buzz cut). I hold a mirror in one hand and the buzzer in the other. So now either the mirror is shaking and I can't see what I'm doing, or the *buzzer* is shaking and I risk losing an ear. If Hollywood brings back the military head shave (circa 1984), I'll be the first boomer on my block to rock it.

I finally had to sell my beloved Vespa. The tremors in my left arm caused the handlebars to shimmy, and the resulting continual swerving of my bike got me pulled over one too many times (much to the delighted merriment of passing drivers) for possible drunk scootering.

If I'm relaxed and warm, the tremor is only slightly noticeable. But if I'm cold, stressed, excited, or just downright pissed off, I shake like a cracked-out seal. Hubs loves this because I can no longer answer the age-old husband question "What's wrong, honey?" with the time-honored humph of "*Nothing.*" He takes one look at my arm flapping like a Three Stooges comedy schtick and says, "You're lying." Kind of takes the sport out of *that* question.

It has long been believed that Parkinson's is not hereditary. Some medical professionals are beginning to rethink this, due to the large percentage of Parkinson's patients with up-line family members with the same disease, but it's still rare for lightening to strike twice in one generation. So I figure *my* getting it reduces my brother and sister's chances to virtually nil. You're welcome, sibs, and don't feel obligated to get me something really expensive for my birthday. Really, you don't have to. Well fine, if you insist.

I decided last year that I wanted to learn to shoot. Hubs bought me a pistol, and we went out to the local Sportsman's Club for some practice.

The cool old guys in their WWII vet hats took one look at my shaking arm, waving a Ruger pistol, and scrambled for cover behind the nearest wooden table. Amid shouts of encouragement and instructions to "Use your GOOD ARM! YOUR GOOD ARM!" they ultimately decided that trap shooting with a shotgun at clay pigeons was probably the safest and most easily controlled option. I'm *totally* hooked.

The old guys tell me there's something called an "open choke" that helps beginners shoot a wider spray, increasing their chances of hitting the clay pigeon. Ha. I just hold up the shotgun, let it wave around the general vicinity, and pull the trigger. Pigeon *down*.

So if you see me on the street and notice the tremor, go ahead. Ask about it. And it's okay to laugh.

"We have two options, medically or emotionally. Give up or fight like hell."

~Lance Armstrong

I AM NOT AMUSED.

Hey Doc,
Call Me When They Find a Cure, Okay?

Several weeks ago, I officially came out on my blog. ("Today I Came Out on My Blog. No, It's Not What You Think.") I'm not gay. I have Parkinson's.

After two years of ignoring the symptoms and telling everyone (including myself) that the tremor in my left hand was simply a pinched nerve, elevating the human ability to deny what we don't want to know to an art form, I finally went to a neurologist, who tossed out "You have Parkinson's disease" like she was ordering a non-fat latte at Starbucks.

Then she added, without looking up from what was either my file or a really fascinating list of biscotti choices, "Oh, there's no cure." Awesome.

Now to say that I'm somewhat resistant to medical intervention is like saying the Kardashian sisters are somewhat partial to swag. Those girls can be bought for free toothpaste, and I'm what doctors in two countries and four states call "non-compliant." I don't keep my appointments, I rarely follow medical advice, and I figure if they can't catch me, they can't tell me what's wrong with me. Yes, I know. Denial is not just a river in Egypt, and my Queen of De Nile tiara has been resolutely attached to my head for 50+ years.

Doc promptly prescribed a little jewel of a pill that only slightly calmed the tremors, but resulted in short-term memory issues at which point I lost my car keys *and* my car, finding them both over an hour later, only to forget where I lived. The third time I rented a movie on Netflix that Hubs and I had already seen the week before, those pills went the way of a dead childhood goldfish. I tossed them. Hubs flushed 'em.

Five years later, even I had to admit this Parkinson's thing wasn't a phase I would simply grow out of like teenage acne, and ignoring it wouldn't make it go away. My mother has had Parkinson's for 25 years (Oh, did I not mention that? Yeah, staring at the symptoms for 20+ years and still able to call it a pinched nerve. Damn, I'm good), and she and Hubs were pushing me hard to get a checkup, preferably at a recognized neurology center rather than simply chatting it up with Cousin Fred's life partner, whose Great-Aunt Agnes had Parkinson's until she discovered kale, which cured her Parkinson's, a nasty neck goiter, and her inability to parallel park. I loved Aunt Agnes.

But by this time, the tremors had become more visible and strangers on the street were starting to ask, "Why is your arm shaking?" (Seriously, people??) I was getting extremely self-conscious about the shaking, so I got the name of the pills my mother was taking for that particular symptom and called my doc for a prescription. I experimented a little with the dosage until I found a daily regimen that helped with the symptoms but didn't cause me to forget the name of the family dog. (Okay, not one of my best plans ever, but anything was preferable to letting the docs get hold of me.)

Then my dad found out.

My stepfather is a retired M.D., who, during his 50+ years of practice, used to run our local hospital and was a past president of the Oregon Medical Association. This is not a man you can ignore. He called my cell phone with a directive to "Come over to the house. Now." Well, crap.

I got there, took one look at his face, and knew my days of denial were over. "Let me see if I've got this right," he stated. "Five years ago, you were diagnosed with a serious, progressive disease, that your mother also has, and since that time, you have not seen one other doctor, have not been to one follow-up appointment, flushed your original prescription down the toilet, and are now taking pills prescribed for your 77-year-old mother, in a dosage you determined was best. Does that about sum things up??"

Well, geez, when you put it like that.

He continued. "I've made an appointment for you at the Oregon Health Sciences University Neurology Center to see a specialist. You will go, and you will listen. If you're going to play doctor, in this game you're the patient. Am. I. Clear?" Crystal, Big Guy. But here's the thing. I know what they're going to say.

"You have Parkinson's." I'm aware of that. I had it five years ago. Still have it. Are you really going to charge me for this?

"There's no cure at this time." Again, aware of that. Gee, do you charge by the hour?

"Here's some pills you can try. They may or may not work on your symptoms. They may or may not also cause severe depression, gas or bloating, or inexplicable rashes up your woo-hoo, which won't really be a problem because they'll obliterate your sex drive, causing all men to suddenly resemble your brother. Oh, and many patients report a significant increase in their appetite." And this just keeps getting better.

"Parkinson's is what we call a 'designer disease,' meaning no two people have exactly the same symptoms or progress at exactly the same rate. We have no idea how this will affect you in the long run." Perfect. And I'm here today why??

"It's kind of a wait-and-see." And there you have it, I said. I was right all along.

Dad looked at me for a long moment, then brought it home with an offer my overachieving, competitive, front-row-of-the-class-that-trophy-is*mine* personality couldn't resist. "What if they can help you?" he asked.

"What if there are options you don't know about that could fix that chicken dance your left arm does all day long? What if you could *fight*?"

By now my mind was whirring with possibilities.

What if?

They say the flip side of denial is anger. That's not true.

It's *hope*.

My appointment is in two weeks. I'm going. And I'm leaving my tiara at home.

"Against the assault of laughter, nothing can withstand."

~Mark Twain

COME TO MAMA

I Finally Met My New Doctor.
Now We're BFFs

Okay, I did it. After two years of total denial, followed by a quick diagnosis and another three years of ignoring it, hoping it would go away on its own like an unexplained rash in your nether regions, finally culminating in several months of self-prescribed medication boosted from my mother's pharmaceutical stash, I caved to family pleadings and agreed to go to Oregon Health Sciences University to see a specialist about my Parkinson's. My M.D. stepfather promptly announced that he was going with me, presumably to keep me from veering off course and hitting up the Nordstrom fall sale and the in-store wine bar instead of the 8th floor at OHSU Neurology. Good call, Dad.

Toting my previous MRI films and a thousand-page questionnaire that now meant some stranger was about 30 minutes from knowing more about me than three husbands, my mother, and the young pup who performed my colonoscopy last year combined, we showed up at the appointed hour and took our seats to wait.

As I looked around, I noticed the place was doing a booming business. Seriously, the entire floor was an undulating sea of shakes and tremors.

I watched for several minutes, ultimately concluding that if you wanted to build a high-rise on a fault line and needed to know if the building was earthquake proof, you could skip the lengthy and expensive scientific testing and just pack the place with a couple hundred Parkinson's patients.

If it can withstand all that rolling, shaking, and swaying for any length of time, you're good to go.

They finally called us in, and I reluctantly went down the hall to meet the doctor who was going to tell me everything I didn't want to hear. Dad's hand was firmly planted on the small of my back to keep my feet pointed *away* from the exit.

The door opened and a pretty, young doc (I'm talking *12*, people. Doogie Howser's little sister) walked in. Baby Doc smiled and said, "I've reviewed your chart, Vikki, and you look quite young," (Gee, I thought, as I flashed her my brightest smile, this might not be so bad after all) until she brought it home with "for a Parkinson's patient." Boom.

"Thanks, Doc," I replied, "But we have a rule in our house about compliments. No qualifiers allowed. And for future reference, 'young for Parkinson's' isn't really a compliment.' Baby Doc burst out laughing and started over, "You look young."

"Thank you," I smiled, "So do you." And people say it's hard to make new friends.

As Baby Doc recited her understanding of the history of my diagnosis and treatment, it was obvious she'd done her homework. I particularly loved her commentary along the way. "So you've never been to another neuro doc in five years? *Seriously*??"

"And you've been taking your mother's Parkinson's meds? *Awesome*." This woman was *funny*, and I loved her.

Confirmation of the original diagnosis was a result of a series of coordination and balance tests, most of which I bombed. 20 minutes later, Baby Doc announces, "Yes, you have Parkinson's." Big surprise. But then she looked right at me and said softly, "I'm sorry."

While I'm not given to wallowing when life throws a curve ball, much preferring the "deny it until you can't, then suck it up and find the funny" approach, I was grateful to have this doc acknowledge, for just a brief second, that this wasn't exactly good news. It was life-changing. It was an unknown, which also made it scary. It was so many, many things at that precise moment.

But it was not *good news*. Her softly spoken apology for this detour in my life was powerful in its simplicity. "I'm sorry." Thank you for that, Baby Doc.

Now on to the fun stuff. The drugs.

There's a virtual cornucopia of Parkinson's medications to choose from, depending upon your age, the duration of your disease, how much medication your body can tolerate, and what side-effects you can live with. Okay, Doc, show me what you've got.

The first pill caused "mild dementia-like symptoms." Bluntly put, you won't remember your own address. I told Baby Doc I was a writer and disinclined to take anything that made me stupid or foggy. Into the "No" pile they sailed.

Next up, great for tremors, but caused "severe edema," particularly in the ankles and calves. Nope, I told her. Hubs is a leg guy. He'll hang in through Parkinson's, but I could lose him over the cankles. "I know," Dad grinned. "Seems shallow, but you can't blame him. She *does* have her mom's legs." What else?

The next little beauties included something for depression, but they commonly caused "rapid weight gain." *Have we met??* I'm not depressed over the Parkinson's, but I'd be borderline suicidal over blowing up like the Hindenburg in three weeks' time. Not gonna happen.

"Yep," drawled Dad, "She's shallow too. What the hell. It works for them."

As we dug through the pile like kids digging under the Christmas tree for presents bearing their names, we tossed out "may cause baldness" (I like my hair short, not gone), "severe night sweats" (already been through menopause. Didn't like it the first time), "genital warts" (oh, *hell* no), "possible addiction to gambling and porn" (we're assuming you didn't have this earlier), until lo and behold, we found a tiny, low-dose marvel whose primary side effect was "decreased appetite and possible anorexia-type symptoms." Well, hot damn. Come to Mama, little one.

30 minutes later, clutching my prescription and my validated parking receipt, we headed for home. I felt okay. Actually, a little better than okay.

I had a Parkinson's buddy. Kind of like a swim buddy at summer camp who promised not to let you drown, but *my* buddy had the ability to take pictures of my brain and give me drugs that made me skinny.

I was instructed to check back in with Baby Doc in one year's time. I think I just might do that.

"Once you choose hope,
anything is possible."

~Anonymous

I'M GOING TO NEED A SECOND OPINION.

Thank You for Searching GoogleDoc.
Yep, You're Gonna Die

Okay. I have a confession to make. I hate sick people. I'm sorry, but I do. They're just so, well...sick. And what's up with the need to share details the rest of us don't need to know (or OMG, visualize, based on your four-color graphic descriptions)?? What you hawked up, how often, what hurts, whether or not you made it to the bathroom before you upchucked the entire burrito sampler platter from the local Taco Truck. When did this become normal conversation? What happened to "How are you?"

"Oh, feeling a bit under the weather, but otherwise fine, thank you"?

I once dumped a guy I liked because he couldn't stop talking about his ongoing sinus infections. Seems he got one on every day that ended with a Y. You know what, Big Guy? I don't even want to know you *have* something called a "sinus," much less that it's usually *infected*. Yes, I know, I'm going to hell.

Then one day, karma came a-calling and I was diagnosed with Parkinson's.

Well, crap.

The first doctor I saw announced my diagnosis with all the interest of a three-year-old at church. "You have Parkinson's," she practically yawned.

"Do you have any questions?" "No thanks," I said on my way out the door, "I'm good." I had about a million questions, but Doc McSleepy wasn't getting any of them. The only thing she didn't do was roll her eyes, and if that happened, I would've immediately leaned over and smacked her with my tremor hand. (Obviously, my newer, more compassionate character remains a work in progress.)

Besides, who needs an actual doctor when you've got the Internet? Like all curious patients of my generation, I immediately went home and fired up every website I could find on Parkinson's. Bad idea. *Bad*.

Medical websites tend to cover every possible outcome, including rare, worst-case scenarios. If anyone in the history of your disease has coughed up a lung, lost an appendage, suddenly become allergic to rice cakes, or, God forbid, died while having it (at age 95), GoogleDoc will end every paragraph with a prediction of your untimely demise.

Typed in "Tremors." Reply: "You're gonna die."

Typed in "Foot cramping." Reply: "You're gonna die."

Tried "Loss of coordination and balance." Reply: "You're not listening.

You're gonna die."

No wonder GoogleDoc is having subscriber issues.

But despite the litigation-induced approach most websites appeared to favor for medical education of the masses, I continued on and GoogleDoc'd my prescription for possible side effects, further proof that humans (okay, me) can dismiss any current, negative experience as an unnecessary consideration when determining whether or not to continue on.

I immediately got a lengthy pop-up list of "It happened to one poor sot in Botswana, so it could happen to you" potential fails that began with, "Many patients experience dementia-like symptoms, temporarily forgetting their addresses, the names of their pets, where they parked their car, and how to perform daily tasks. We recommend cue cards."

Awesome. Now I'm supposed to spend next Saturday drawing little stick figures pulling on their underwear, lest I inadvertently leave the house on a windy day while going commando under my skirt.

It continued, "And be sure to call your doctor right away if you experience uncontrollable weight gain, nausea or projectile vomiting, constipation lasting more than a month, facial tics or paralysis, genital warts, water retention like a two-humped camel, tearing of your vaginal mesh, complete obliteration of your sex drive, voices in your head, visible back fat, or sudden death." (I'm assuming here that if I'm actually dead, that last one would be for my next of kin, but what the hell. By now, who cares?)

And if you're not quite depressed enough by now to get off your computer and head to the kitchen for a quart of Chunky Monkey Sundae ice cream and a bottle of Zin, self-appointed experts suggest you start a daily journal documenting the progression of your symptoms and what activities you can no longer do. Oh. Dear. God. What idiot thought that was a good idea?? So I'm supposed to get up every morning and review what Parkinson's is doing to my body and what activities I used to enjoy, but can never do again? I call this the "Anti-Gratitude Journal," or more aptly, "How to go From Depressed to Suicidal in 60 Seconds a Day."

Oh, hell no.

Ultimately, I decided to find another doctor, ban all computer searches on Parkinson's disease (excluding michaeljfox.org and thebarrow.com, where hope, compassion, and the belief in a cure sooner rather than later makes these my go-to sites for all things Parkinson's), and I'm starting a daily journal about what I *can* do.

Day 1:

1: Yep, I could die, but it hasn't happened yet. I can work with that.

2: I can laugh. Medical experts are quick to call Parkinson's a "lifelong battle." I figure as long as I'm laughing, it hasn't even won the skirmish, much less the war.

3: I can love. And if my beloved puppy has to wear a "Hello, My Name is Paco" tag, so be it.

4: I can dance. Yes, it's goofy, but it always was.

5. I can write. My greatest passion remains intact.

And maybe someday I'll write a book about my journey. I promise, it'll make you laugh. Until then, my journal is waiting. Today, I'm gonna dance.

"I believe that laughter is the best emotional Band-Aid in the world. It's like nature's Neosporin."

~Matt LeBlanc

Medication Madness.
When Even Your Prescription Has a Prescription

When my son, Jake, was young, we had many talks, like most families, about drugs and the dangers they bring. One day he brought a magazine over to me and dropped it into my lap. He opened a page to show me a large ad for a brightly colored pill being held up by a beaming woman like it was The Answer to smoother skin, thinner thighs, and world peace.

Then he turned the page to show me the description of the possible side effects, written in four-point type and roughly the length of a master's thesis.

"Isn't that a drug?" he asked.

"Why is it okay?" I explained that medications are designed by doctors to help people get better when they're sick, but that all drugs, medicines or otherwise, have side effects. "That's a lot of bad stuff for something that's supposed to help," he replied. Welcome to my world, 15 years later.

Since being diagnosed with Parkinson's, half-a-dozen doctors and I have been searching for the right medications and the right dosages for symptomatic relief. It's been a bit of a bumpy ride.

There are several choices a Parkinson's patient has when deciding on a medication. Parkinson's is a very individual disease. Everyone has it a little differently, manifesting slightly different symptoms and progressing at different rates. Understandably, this makes it difficult to treat. Remember that at this time, there are no cures, just possible relief from the annoying and often embarrassing shaking, tremors, rolling motions, and balance issues.

We're given choices, in terms of results vs. side effects, and dosages are often in a wide range that we ultimately determine for ourselves through trial and error. This is not, "Here's your antibiotic. Take two every morning with breakfast, at this fixed dosage, for one week." It's more "Let's try this one. Start with 1 mg., then add one more every few days until your symptoms are reduced. You should settle in somewhere between 6 and 24 mg. Oh, and side effects could include extreme lethargy, premature baldness, uncontrollable weight gain, a sudden desire to gamble, hallucinations, cankles, adult-onset acne, or chronic insomnia. But it should reduce your hand tremors. You wanna give it a try?"

It's of note that the women in my family are extremely prone to side effects of medications. Over the years, we've each sat in doctors' offices for one reason or another and heard, "Well, the reaction *you're* experiencing is extremely rare, but yes, it's possible."

If there's even a *slight* chance (on par with, say, winning the lottery, while getting struck by lightning) that the pill I popped at breakfast might cause increased back fat, hair-trigger moodiness, or a sudden need to hit the casinos with all our savings, Hubs just stays out of my way and changes the passwords on our bank accounts, because one or more of those "rare" side effects will roll over me like a runaway Mac truck.

Cases in point:

Prescription #1. This one caused what I can only describe as early dementia. I couldn't remember what I had for breakfast on any given day.

I was constantly bringing home movies we'd seen the previous week, with absolutely no memory of ever watching them. I'd ask Hubs a question, and he'd look confused, then reply, "We just had this conversation yesterday."

One evening after work, I walked for blocks looking for where I parked my car that morning. I finally called Hubs and wailed, "I can't find my car. I think it's been stolen."

There was a brief silence, and he said, slowly, "I took you to work this morning. Don't you remember?" That night, the pills were tossed.

Prescription #2. The second little wonder was for the dystonia, which sounds kind of pretty until you realize that "dys" before any word means "*something's* wrong." Dystonia is severe muscle cramping, in my case in my foot. It happened every morning, usually on the right, with my toes curling under, causing that foot to become instantly non-weight-bearing. For the next 30-45 minutes, I'd have to get around the house hopping on one foot while shaking the other like a dog after a tree pee, trying to get it to release. Rx #2 also caused such dry mouth that I often couldn't swallow or speak distinctly. (Apparently you need saliva to keep your mouth and tongue forming words over your teeth. Who knew?) New acquaintances just assumed I had Parkinson's *and* a speech impediment. Next.

Prescription #3. Made me as nocturnal as an alley cat. Every night around 2 a.m., I'd tap Hubs awake, wearing nothing but an enthusiastic tremor and a smile. The first few nights, he was positively giddy. By the fifth night, he groaned and mumbled, eyes still closed, "Geez, sweetie. It's been four nights in a row. I'm too old for this. I need *sleep*." (To be fair, being regularly descended upon at 2 a.m. by a human vibrator with no Off switch and a tendency to topple off the bed in all but the most secure positions loses a bit of its magic by the fifth consecutive night. One could hardly blame an occasional pass.)

Two weeks later, I was bleary-eyed from sleep deprivation. Doc offered another prescription, purely designed to counteract the side effects of the original prescription, but I was reluctant to embrace the approach that treats medication issues with more medication. Whoever said "Better living through pharmaceuticals" was an idiot. Moving on.

Prescription #4. Next up was a tiny little thing that promised "possible rapid weight loss." (Well, where have you been, little one?? Yes, I'm shallow. Don't judge.) It virtually eliminated my tremors, and I felt great.

Then one night I opened my eyes and saw a man in a black hoodie at the end of the bed. I started screaming, and Hubs was yelling, "What's wrong? *What's wrong?!?*" I pointed, "There's a man in our room! See?? That man!" Hubs grabbed my hands and repeated, several times, "There's *no one there*."

The next day, I made some phone calls and discovered that three percent (yeah, big surprise, that would include me) of patients who take this drug experience hallucinations. Seriously?? We tried lowering the dosage, but it didn't help.

Every night, I'd see people in the bedroom, in the closets, or down the hall, and I'd hear footsteps and conversations all throughout the house.

After a week or so, I started talking back. Hubs decided it was too late for me to experience the psychedelic '60s for the first time, so they hit the "No" pile.

We're now trying a new drug that seems to be promising, with only minor side effects so far.

Someday they'll find a cure for this disease. I'm hoping it will be in my lifetime. Then all this will just be a memory for my grandchildren about the time Grandma had imaginary friends.

Part 2

Finding the Funny

"Laughter is the sensation of feeling good all over and showing it principally in one place."

~Josh Billings

And They Said it Wouldn't Last

Hubs and I graduated from high school together in 1974 (ouch!), and although he was my brother's best friend at the time, we never dated, and in fact, rarely socialized.

Hubs was a star athlete, with a bad boy side, and I was an overachieving pleaser, with decidedly prissy tendencies (think Rachel on *Glee*. Without the voice.) While he was scoring yet another touchdown in front of the entire cheering town and out making a rebel name for himself in three counties, I was at home, practicing my glide walk (books on head, shoulders back, eyes forward, and *smile*) on stage for the local Junior Miss pageant. Suffice it to say, our paths were not destined to cross for several years.

Fast forward to our 25th high school reunion. Oh my. We were married 18 months later, and have since discovered that a lot can happen to a person in 25 years. Hubs is a funny, generous, extremely loyal man, passionate about his family, committed to his work, and his Harley sports an American flag in honor of our son, who is in the military.

Hub's wife (yeah, that would be me) has undiagnosed ADHD with OCD tendencies, can't cook or back up a car, can only work the stilettos in the bedroom (if I don't have to actually walk), while more likely to be found in sweats (preferably his). She's a *terrible* nurse when he's sick, routinely sets the house on fire, uses the naked shimmy dance as a way of apologizing (while freely admitting that over the years, it has become more goofy than sexy), and has a passion for red wine, but usually has more of it down her shirt than in her glass. Then I got Parkinson's, handing him a couple of decades of watching his wife trip over her Reeboks on a daily basis and shake like an excited zoo seal every morning until her meds kick in.

To sum it all up, one of us got hosed.

Our local newspaper, like many small-town papers, likes to report extensively on the doings of community members, including a section called "YesterYears," which reports highlights from 10-50 years ago.

(What I remember most about our little paper in those early years is that they reported who was in the local hospital, why they were there, what room they were in, and whether or not they were receiving visitors. Awesome. I just aged myself like a billion years. This was obviously when HIPAA was a large African water mammal. Our senior class regularly had wheelchair races down the Emergency Room hallway every Saturday Kids today haven't lived.)

So I'm out running errands and come home to find Hubs in a fit of uncontrolled mirth, clutching the Hood River News. When I asked why such unabashed hilarity, he gleefully pointed to the YesterYears section, which mentioned my graduation from the local high school's Charm School course in 1973. "You went to CHARM SCHOOL??" he choked out. "WHAT HAPPENED???"

He's gone to the store, giving me just enough time to charmingly stuff all his crap into the guest room.

"You don't stop laughing
because you grow old.
You grow old because
you stop laughing."

~Michael Pritchard

HOW OLD ARE YOU ANYWAY?

Not Sure if You're Getting Older?
Here's Your Sign

Recently, a friend asked me if she could post a photo of me on her Facebook page. Although we've been friends for years and there are very few things she could ask of me that I wouldn't cheerfully hand over (money, my favorite dress, a kidney), I found myself saying no to the photo.

I hate pictures of myself. My hair is so blonde it doesn't show up against any light background, so I look like a bald hoot owl in most head shots, AND no matter what we tell ourselves about how young we still look, *pictures don't lie.* Every line, droop, softening, missed workout, diet relapse, or one-too-many glasses of wine is hanging out there, in full glossy color, announcing to the world what we can't admit to ourselves.

We're getting *old.*

I know what you're thinking. "It's how you *feel* that counts." "You're only as old as you think you are." "Beauty is what's on the *inside.*" Yeah, yeah, yeah. But all that internal beauty and youthful thinking is housed inside a body that has seen better days, and some days we get not-so-subtle reminders that time is marching on.

How to tell if you're getting older?

1. You see a picture of yourself and realize that what everybody says is true. You look exactly like your mother. Granted, your mother may be beautiful (yes, Mom, you are), but she's *20 years older than you.* There's a difference between "having your mother's smile" and "looking like your mother."

2. When you wake up in the morning, the pillow creases on your face haven't gone away by the time you leave for work *two hours later.*

3. Your grandchildren (let's just start with the fact that you *have* grandchildren) like to pull your hand skin up and giggle hysterically at how long it takes to go back down.

4. You acknowledge people on the street with a smile and a head nod, because your once-defined triceps now flap like sheets on a clothesline whenever you lift your arms to wave.

5. You own Spanx but never wear them, because you can no longer bend over far enough to pull them on.

6. You remember the "pencil test" to determine if your backside is drooping, but now you can get three yellow highlighters under one cheek and hold them there all day.

7. Body parts move when you're standing still. Boobs sway, butts jiggle, thighs ripple. If we could get it all synchronized, we could YouTube a new dance meme, but unfortunately, boobs tend to swing east and west, butts go south, and thighs have a mind of their own. God has a wicked sense of humor.

8. Every year you have to eat less to maintain the same weight. (At this rate, I figure by 2020, my daily food allowance will be one fruit loop and a Diet Coke.)

9. You start looking at wine as possibly "empty calories" and wonder if you should cut back. (But then that inner youthful exuberance makes you burst out with "Bahahahaha!!!" You're old. Not dead.)

10. You get diagnosed with what you always thought of as an "old person's" disease, that you'll spend the next few decades trying to outrun. Parkinson's, cancer, dementia. Conditions your parents and their friends might be living with suddenly start hitting three-quarters of your high school reunion roster.

Last weekend I was playing with a friend's five-year-old daughter, tickling and giggling, when she announced, "*Your* hands are way older than mommy's!"

"Oh?" I choked out. "Uh-huh," she nodded. "And hers don't shake like yours. Yep," she insisted, as she looked up and peered closely at my face, "You're *definitely* old."

My friendship with her only-slightly-younger mother is all that stood between me and an overwhelming urge to toss the future tramp off the balcony. So if I don't post next week, you can assume I've passed on in my sleep. What the hell. They'll say I had a good run.

"With mirth
and laughter,
let the
old wrinkles come."

~William Shakespeare

Date Night.
This Isn't How I Remember It.

Recently, I was reading an article called "10 Ways to Bring Back the Romance in Your Marriage." I immediately showed it to Hubs and asked him, smiling, "What do you think? Should we try some of these?"

He instantly got that panicked looked he reserves for conversations of this nature, undoubtedly imagining the 101 things he *didn't* want to do to put the spice back in a marriage he thinks is fine just the way it is.

Let's start with #3, I suggested. It's simple. Make a Date Night, like we did when we were, well...dating. You know, get dressed up, go out to a romantic restaurant, gaze into each other's eyes like besotted fools, spend several hours reassuring each other of our mutual, eternal love, then go home and make passionate love all night long, finally curling up together like a human corkscrew, falling asleep in a state of Phase 1 bliss. Hubs looked over and surprised me with "Sure. Why not?"

Well, hot damn.

Mama's going on a date.

First task: Pick a night. Saturday? Nope, kids are coming for the weekend.

Okay. The next one? Can't do it. Working all weekend. Fine. The one after *that*? Uh-uh. That's your annual golf trip. For heaven's sake. The one after *that*?? It'll work?? Great.

Next, pick a restaurant. "How about the Mexican restaurant?"

"Not a chance," Hubs replied, "The last time I ate there, it took me three days to digest the giant cheeseball stuck in my intestines." (Yeah, no romance needed here.)

"Okay, then. How about Thai food?"

"Don't know what that is," he stated, "and if I don't recognize it, I'm not eating it."

"Fine. We like that one downtown with the deck and the great view. How about that?"

"Isn't that the place that serves those complimentary crab thingies? I threw up all night, remember?" Could've done without that visual, but okay, crab cakes are out.

"Let's just settle for the historic hotel, with dinner out on the patio. Deal?" Done.

Now, what to wear?

As I perused my closet, it became clear that my clothing choices had become less about "dancing till they shut this party down" and more about "can I machine wash this after my baby granddaughter pees on it?"

I ransacked my wardrobe, trying on everything I thought might work, but it became rapidly clear that over the years, as my boobs got longer and my butt got wider, my necklines went up and my skirt lengths went down, until I was starting to resemble my Great-Aunt Agnes from Idaho, only without the unfortunate under-eye mole and hair snood.

"Where are you going?" Hubs asked, as I grabbed my purse and headed out the door. "Shopping," I said, "I have *nothing* to wear for Date Night."

"I knew it," I heard him mumble to himself, "We haven't even *left* yet and it's already costing us a ton of money."

A trip to my favorite boutique quickly unearthed a fabulous (albeit widely overpriced) black jumpsuit, with sexy, slightly-off-the-shoulder sleeves and elegant wide-leg pants. Trying to ignore the tiny voice in my head that said this was actually just a grown-up onesie, I plunked down our credit card with barely enough time for the salesclerk to ask, brightly, "So, what shoes will you be wearing?" Oh, crap.

Mentally reviewing my current shoe wardrobe, I knew that I had nothing that would work. Over the years, balance issues from Parkinson's had systematically eliminated my stiletto cache, making room for low platforms and sneakers, neither of which scream "Come get me, Big Guy."

Date Night required heels. The kind even *he* knows you can't walk in for more than three steps. And let's get real here. Those shoes weren't actually made for *walking*. They're for showing off in the bedroom.

The dilemma was multifold.

1) I hadn't worn heels for years, and they require practice to prevent comic, albeit humiliating and decidedly unsexy pratfalls or sprained ankles.

2) My right foot is given to spontaneous bouts of dystonia, which simply means it cramps up, instantly becoming non-weight-bearing and necessitating hopping on my left foot to my destination until it wears off, say, 30 to 45 minutes later. Parkinson's doctors don't know for sure what triggers this, but it's safe to say that the pitch of stilettos will get you there before Hubs can whisper "Who's your Daddy?"

And 3) The sight of me strutting my middle-age stuff in nothing but high heels in the bedroom would undoubtedly send Hubs into gales of uncontrollable laughter or screaming for an eye-wash station. I finally compromised with a pair of strappy silver sandals with a high wedge. Not exactly stilettos, but compared to my old PayLess sneakers, he'll love them.

Then finally, the big night arrived.

Sitting at the restaurant, looking over the wine list, Hubs looked up and said, "Have you seen these prices?? Who the hell pays $100 for a bottle of wine??"

"I agree," I said. "That's not us. Check out the *entrée* prices."

"You know," he said, "for the price of this dinner, we could get the shelving for the pantry."

"That's true," I replied. "And the kids called today. They need to borrow some money."

"Are you thinking what I'm thinking?" he asked.

"Yep," I said. "Let's ditch this place and go get chips and a pitcher of margaritas at the taco stand."

Four hours later, faces hurting from laughing and non-stop talking over too many margaritas and three bowls of guacamole, we stumbled out of the cab and into the house, heading down the hall to the bedroom.

"Tonight was so much fun," I said. "But I'm really tired. Would you mind if we didn't..."

"Oh thank God," he replied. "I'm exhausted. Can we schedule that for next weekend?"

It was a perfect evening. And I still have the shoes.

"Never give up on things
that make you smile."

~Anonymous

TRY POLE DANCING, THEY SAID,
IT'S EASY, THEY SAID.

I Gave Hubs a Pole Dance and He Can't Stop Laughing.
It's Been Two Days

After the success of our date night, recommended in the article "10 Ways to Bring Back the Romance in Your Marriage," I thought I'd pick another suggestion for this week. #4 was "Try something sexy and fun that you've never done before." As my mind began a quick visual reel of possibilities, I immediately ruled out naked tandem bungee jumping or partner swapping (unless I get Robert Redford and Hubs takes the homeless woman under the bridge), and finally settled on one of the author's ideas. I decided to learn to pole dance.

I know what you're thinking. This probably wasn't the obvious choice. Yes, I'm aware that I'm 57, I've never done this before, my gene pool leans more towards sturdy German peasant stock than limber Romanian gymnast, and I have Parkinson's. What the hell. Go big or go home, as they say. I promptly ordered a "Pole Dancing for Beginners" DVD and eagerly awaited the lessons on how to wow my man.

Of course, figuring out the *pole* part of the kit was a bit tougher. This isn't something you can just order and have delivered with no questions asked, especially when you live in a small town. When the UPS guy that you dated in high school asks "What's new with you?" as he delivers your porn pole, he *really* wants to know.

Three days later, my DVD arrived, and I immediately popped it in, ready to get started rockin' Hubs' world.

Since I didn't have an actual pole, I decided to improvise with the wooden pillar that separates the kitchen from the living room. Silently offering up a prayer that "weight bearing" was meant literally, I grabbed hold with both hands and prepared to execute my first exotic dance move.

1. The Wrap-Around. Grab the pole. Stick one leg out, swing it to the side, step and pivot (bending the knee to make it more graceful), hook the pole with your outside foot, and finish by arching your back. Yeah, no.

I grabbed the pole with one hand, swung a leg out to the side, whacking my foot on the indoor ficus, stepped and pivoted, twisting my ankle as I hooked the pole, then limped on to the Big Finish, energetically arching my back and swinging one arm up overhead, immediately causing a nasty back spasm, accompanied by repeated, involuntary yelps of "Owee, owee,

owee!" Okay, then. Apparently we need less enthusiasm, more technique.

2. The Basic Climb. This is the stripper version of rope climbing in 8th grade P.E. class, but in less clothes. Since I was unsure whether the thin wooden pillar would withstand my 120-pound attempt to mount it, I decided to improvise and try a door casing.

Blithely ignoring the tremor in my left arm and the chronic, medication-induced foot spasms, I grabbed hold of the bathroom door jamb and began my ascent.

Note to self: When you need two arms and two legs to do something, and only one of each works with any consistency, consider skipping that exercise.

Thirty seconds later, I was a tangled heap on the floor, mortified as I realized that all the blinds were open and the delighted neighbors were gathering in the driveway to watch the show.

3. The Fireman Spin. Ha. I've got this one *down*. Small leap, grab the pole, bend the knees, and let centrifugal force spin you repeatedly around the pole until you stick the landing with *small* back arch and a flourish of the arm. Piece of cake. Until I flourished before I stopped spinning. I spun off the pole and into the front door, cracking my head on the door knob.

Yeah, that'll leave a mark.

4. The Body Wave. Basically a full-body undulation, while hanging onto the pole with one arm and leaning out. Like most Parkinson's patients,

I struggle a little with coordination activities, specifically like my body waving in *one* direction and my arm going in *another*. It looked less like an erotic pole dance and more like I was frantically flagging down an ambulance on a deserted street. Moving on.

5. The Backwards Wiggle. Stand up with your back to the pole, grab said pole with hands up behind your head, then gyrate your hips as you slide down. Seriously??

First of all, I'm not built for gyrating. I couldn't gyrate in college, when I was considerably younger, 15 pounds thinner, and my appendages only shook when I told them to. All attempts at gyrating simply looked like I'd just been tasered. But I did discover that when I put my hands up behind my head, it inexplicably increased the tremors, resulting in a fairly impressive shimmy. This one could work. It's all about making lemonade, people.

So that evening when Hubs came home, I proudly announced my new secret skill. Not surprisingly, he was thrilled and immediately settled in, happily anticipating my Big Move. I decided on the Fireman Spin, letting my body weight do most of the work. I grabbed the pole, swung out my leg to get a good spin going, tucked the other heel up under my butt, and flashed my brightest "Come Get Me, Sailor" smile as I twirled past him.

On the second twirl, my foot cramped up and my arm had a seismic tremor that caused me to let go of the pole and sail across the room, landing on top of an unexpecting Hubs with a thud, sending him into unrestrained laughter, while he choked out, "That was *awesome*. Do it again!"

He still thinks it was supposed to be like that. I'm not telling him otherwise. But I'm thinking of teaching a pole dancing class at the next Parkinson's convention. We've still got the moves.

"Courage doesn't always roar.
Sometimes courage
is the quiet voice at the
end of the day, saying,
I will try again
tomorrow."

~Mary Anne Radmacher

IT'S OKAY.
TOMORROW WE'LL
BOTH TRY AGAIN.

Maybe I Should've Bought a Bird

Several years ago, shortly after we moved into our house, I decided to buy Hubs a dog. When we were renting, our landlord had a firm "No Dogs. Ever" policy. But Hubs had grown up with dogs, and I knew he missed having a canine companion. Since we're both fairly OCD about our house, a short-haired, small breed seemed more practical. I searched around and finally found an adorable light tan Chihuahua puppy, and promptly plunked down $400 to take her home. Hubs fell in love before I even got her completely out of her little leopard print tote bag, when all he could see was her oversized fruit-bat ears and enormous brown eyes.

A few months later, she was up to 14 pounds. We took her to the vet, where Hubs held her up like baby Simba in *The Lion King* and asked Dr. Dave, "Is this a Chihuahua?"

Doc cracked up. "Nope. That's what you call a 'Rat-Cha.' She's part Chihuahua, which would explain the giant ears, but mostly she's a Rat Terrier."

"But we paid $400 for a Chihuahua," Hubs said.

"Then you got hosed," Doc replied, "because that's a Rat Terrier. And you can get one for about 50 bucks."

What the hell. By that time, Hubs and Chi-Chi were besotted with each other and she ran the house.

Since Chi-Chi was without question Hubs' dog, I decided to get a pup of my own. A month later, I happily brought home a real Chihuahua named Paco. He's a sturdy (okay, fat) little guy that lives to eat, sleep, and cuddle.

Hubs says he's completely useless ("May as well have a *cat*," he points out with only slightly annoying regularity). I've tried every doggie diet plan I can think of, but since he's arguably the most sedentary dog on the planet, he burns roughly 10 calories a day, while sharing my passion for cinnamon rolls and Cheez-in-a-Can.

The one thing that will get Paco off his hairless hind-end is the neighbor's cat, Pippy. Pippy is twice Paco's size and runs like a Cheetah, but she can get Paco going like nobody's business. Why he thinks he can catch her, and exactly what he's going to do with her if he does, will forever remain a mystery, particularly since she could kick the crap out of him with one paw tied behind her back.

One morning, Pippy strolled across our yard, waving her over-fluffed tail to make sure Paco saw her, and it was Game On. Paco tore out of the house as fast as his short, chubby little legs would go, while Pippy bent low and sprang into action to lead the chase.

I dropped my breakfast and raced out, wearing nothing but bunny slippers and a pink bathrobe, chasing Paco across the grade-school soccer field next to our house. (Did I forget to mention he's not the smartest dog in the kennel and can't remember where he lives if he gets farther than two houses away? Simply put, if you can't see him, he can't find you.)

Normally the soccer field is pretty much empty in the mornings, so I wasn't particularly concerned about running into anyone (literally or otherwise), naked under my robe, as I chased down my tiny, but admirably determined puppy.

Unfortunately, my Parkinson's symptoms are in high gear first thing in the morning. My right foot cramps and rolls underneath itself, essentially becoming non-weight-bearing for the next 45 minutes or so, making it virtually impossible to run unless I put most of my weight on the left foot and just use the cramping foot to add a little hop. And in those same morning hours, my tremor arm shakes like I'm whipping imaginary cake batter. But knowing that Paco could easily get too far away to find his way home, I had no choice but to go after him.

As I skip-hopped as fast as I could go (skip, skip, hop; skip, skip, hop) trying to maintain my balance while clutching my bathrobe to keep it closed (seriously, what I had under there was not something most people wanted to see at seven in the morning or, let's be honest, ever), yelling for my little guy to give it up and come home, three things suddenly became clear.

Fact #1: Dogs can't catch cats.

Fact #2: Even if mastering the foot cramp skip-hop, middle-aged women with Parkinson's, especially while wearing nothing but a bathrobe and oversize bunny slippers, can't catch dogs chasing cats.

Fact #3: My neighbors love to be entertained at my expense and will often migrate in the direction of the current commotion, cheering and laughing over their morning coffee, waving as I flew by in a pink, skippy blur.

I'm usually perfectly willing to offer up my personal humiliations for entertainment purposes (Have you read my blog?), but on some mornings, it appears that my sole purpose in life is to provide anyone within a two-block radius a daily chuckle and a story that would be embellished over the dinner table ("I heard she was *naked*") by people that weren't even there. My only hope for help were the two 18-year-old studs we blew past, who might have stepped up if they weren't doubled over laughing.

Two blocks later, Pippy's vanished and I skip/hopped home, carrying my exhausted, defeated pup. Don't feel bad, little guy. She'll be back tomorrow.

"Laughter is
an instant vacation."

~Milton Berle

Can I Just Order Cold Pizza To Go?

Hubs was out running an early-morning errand, so I decided on cold Hawaiian pizza from last night's dinner for breakfast. It's my undisputed favorite "If you were choosing your last meal, what would it be?" breakfast. Throw in a couple of frosted brownies with walnuts, and I'm ready to face the hereafter.

My criteria for any hot pizza is how it will taste cold, the next morning. Many (oh, so many. I didn't get this body from carrot sticks) have been tried; few have been chosen. But we had lunch at our favorite pizzeria in Portland the day before, purposely ordering large sizes so I'd have breakfasts for the next several days. Grabbing a plate, I happily cut two generous slices, unknowingly dropping a small cube of pineapple onto the kitchen floor.

One of the first signs of Parkinson's for many people is a visible decline in balance and coordination. Simply put, we can trip over virtually any object, no matter how hard to detect, regularly leaving us in embarrassing, tangled heaps on the floor, that may or may not require assistance from the next person coming through the door.

As I turned towards the table, I stepped on the slippery little fruit guy, shooting one leg out in a front split and the other out in a side split (neither of which God built me to do), toppling the rest of my body forward, frantically waving my arms towards the counter for stability, managing only to smack the edge of my plate, tossing loaded pizza slices into the air (and since what goes *up*, must come *down*), crashing me and the entire mess (tomato sauce in my hair?? REALLY??) onto the floor in an extremely undignified pile, ironically achieving a Reverse Plow position no amount of instruction from my long-suffering yoga instructor has ever been able to manage, while simultaneously providing unrestricted viewing of limbs that haven't seen a razor since last October. (It's *winter*, people. If you can't see it, I'm not shaving it).

With perfect marital timing, Hubs came home and walked in to see me sprawled on the kitchen floor, lying on my back like an upended beetle, covered with Canadian bacon and pineapple, blinking up at him through bits of melted cheese (Note to self: next time, skip the extra toppings).

As I waited to hear his first comment, my mind did a mash-up slideshow of the times he's come home to caved-in garage ceilings, dryer fires, buzz-sawed yard plants, tire tracks in the grass, prematurely ripped up house flooring, screaming smoke alarms going off in the kitchen, and an incensed neighbor the day I accidentally took out his customized mailbox (although in my defense, the "customizing" he was so inexplicably proud of was simply a replica of that stupidly popular singing fish plaque you see on QVC at 2 a.m. Here's 30 bucks. Buy a new one), so I wasn't quite sure where he'd go with this one.

He took a long look and announced, "Unless you're hurt, DON'T TELL ME. I don't want to know." Then he calmly stepped over me and continued down the hall. My first thought was, "Hey buddy! A little help here??"

Then I decided he's right. Some things are better left alone.

"Mix a little foolishness
with your prudence.
It's good to be silly at the
right moment."

~Horace (Roman lyric poet)

I LOVE SCIENCE!!!

Studies Also Show That Red Wine is Good For You.
I Knew That

One of my favorite magazines has a "Miscellaneous Good Stuff" section, where I find all kinds of cool, albeit questionably true trivia like "Did you know that rubbing used coffee grounds on your thighs reduces cellulite?" Notwithstanding the four times Hubs found me in the bathroom with his Mr. Coffee, dumping his morning grounds all over my legs and scrubbing them with the hopeful enthusiasm of a 9-year-old rubbing a magic genie lamp (I'm a sucker for anything that promises to make me younger, thinner, or taller, with only nominal effort on my part), I'm usually mildly skeptical. But then again, unless it mentions sudden death or increased back fat as possible side effects, I pretty much always end up at "No guts, no glory. Let's give it a try."

This month's gem stated "Studies show that if you use your non-dominant hand for common daily tasks, it makes you smarter." Okay, why not? I like smart. Smart is good.

I'm right-handed, so I shifted every task I could think of over to my left hand, and even made a list of things to try, including a few suggestions provided in the article. Keep in mind that my left hand is not only non-dominant, it's the one with the Parkinson's tremor. This promised to be, if not an actual scientific study, at least an entertaining experiment. And if you read my blog, you know that I have somewhere near zero reservations about offering up my personal humiliations for public amusement, so I was in. Full steam ahead, damn the consequences, as they say. (Okay, I say that. A lot more than Hubs would like, but that's another post altogether.)

Experiment #1: Eat with your left hand. Thank God I was home alone.

Grabbed a fork and spent the next two minutes trying to guide my noncompliant tremor hand into the general direction of my plate, until I finally managed to stab a macaroni elbow, hopefully securing it on the fork tines long enough to get it to my mouth.

Reminiscent of playing "Here comes the airplane" with my toddler years ago, the next step was getting the fork and the noodle, with my hand now shaking like an over-excited baby seal, back up to my mouth.

Four tries later, with two macaroni noodles in my hair and half a dozen tremor-launched onto the floor or down the front of my shirt, it appeared I was going to starve to death, until surprisingly, I hit my target. Sort of. I had two noodles in my mouth. I also stabbed myself in the lip and on my cheek, bleeding all over my fork and confirming my suspicion that I am definitely too old to rock a facial piercing. But not being one to dwell on failure, I simply conceded defeat on this particular exercise and moved on.

#2: Blow-dry your hair. Ha. This was almost too easy. The tremor arm is unparalleled for keeping the blow-dryer moving, thus avoiding frying your hair. It's true that at some point my arm got tired before my hair was totally dry and I ended up with a new part and sporting a weird cowlick that no amount of wind-tunnel-tested hair gel would tame, but it was close enough to my original style, so I called that one a win. Don't judge.

#3. Sign your name. With my left hand?? C'mon, people. Most non-Parkinson's patients can't do this and make it legible. But in the spirit of the Great Experiment, I was willing to give it a try. Grabbed a pen and wrote "Vikki Claflin" 15 times with my shaking hand, trying to produce a signature that was legible to anyone other than me and possibly to my husband. Ironically, the more tired my arm gets, the more it shakes, so each signature was slightly less legible than the one above it. Ultimately, they all looked like "Virgin Clapping," which would never hold up in contract court, and handwriting profilers will forever claim I'm a serial killer.

#4. Text something sexy to your hubs. By now I was starving, I had bed hair, and my voter registration card had been revoked for questionable signatures. But this one could make it all worthwhile.

I spent the next 20 minutes trying to hammer out a sexy text message with a tired, but still shaky hand, mentally hurtling the inventor of autocorrect to hell on a luge with every word it auto-inserted that I didn't want (If I wanted to say "noodle," I would've typed "noodle," you moron. For the eighteenth time, it's "nooky." N-O-O-K-Y. Seriously, guy, get it in your Rolodex, okay??)

By the time I was done, I was ready to send a decidedly unsexy text to Mr. Auto-Correct and I'd lost the mood, but I'm also too OCD to leave the assignment incomplete, so I kept tapping until I finally had something I felt was hot and witty to surprise Hubs.

At that moment, I had a Parkinson's tremor-jerk (instead of small, rapid shakes, it's a strong, involuntary arm flail that could take out the décor on a coffee table in one shot) while tapping out the phone number, prematurely hitting "Send" before I could double-check the digits, irretrievably cyber-sailing my hoochie text to some guy I don't even know. Uh-oh. I'm guessing my new friend Bubba has a wee history of playing outside the marital sandbox, because I immediately got a frantic reply, "STOP TEXTING. WIFE IS HOME." Bad Bubba. Bad.

So now my I.Q. is up two points, but my face needs stitches, my checks won't clear the bank, and apparently I'm being named in a divorce suit between two people I've never met.

But I'm taking a win on the blow-dryer.

I am careful not to confuse excellence with perfection. Excellence, I can reach for. Perfection is God's business.

~Michael J. Fox

OH WAITER. MORE WINE PLEASE.

Thanks for the Compliment.
Now Stop Talking

Out on the town for our weekly Thursday night wine tour, Hubs and I checked the local winery map and spotted one we hadn't tried yet, that boasted several awards for their reds. (Have you ever noticed that every winery on the planet has won "Winery of the Year" and has multiple bottles draped in medals for "Best Cab," "Best Pinot Noir," or "Best Chardonnay" proudly displayed on their back-bar like soldiers in formation? I'm thinking the wine committee is made up of soccer parents who believe every kid should win an award just for participating.) But who cares? The tasting room was very log cabiny, with a floor-to-ceiling rustic rock fireplace, popping and crackling, and providing some serious romantic ambiance designed to get you to hang out for a while, so we happily cozied up to the bar for some sampling.

As we were sharing some of their "award-winning" Syrah (okay, I'll give them this one. It was fabulous), chatting about our day, I suddenly noticed Hubs staring at me with an odd expression on his face. I was smack in the middle of a truly fascinating story about who said what on Twitter. But since Hubs abhors technology, I assumed he'd lost the sliver of interest he had in my subject or maybe I just had a big piece of spinach in my teeth from the complimentary dip tray. Either way, it shut me up mid-sentence, at which point he smiled and said, "I was just thinking how pretty you are."

Well, gee thanks! Feeling all girly and loved, I flashed him my flirtiest "Yes, you did get lucky, Big Fella" smile, while I ordered another round. (I was liking the way this conversation was going. Let's stay for another glass.)

Unfortunately, he continued...

"It's not like you're a movie star or anything, or have a 25-year-old hard body.

I mean, I used to play football and you used to be a cheerleader. We both know those days are gone forever, huh?" (My smile was starting to feel a little pasted on.) "And now here we are. You're 57 with Parkinson's, and my football glory days are just a vague memory that I can embellish all I want because we're all too old to remember." Okay. I've now moved past the pasted smile and gone directly to "How many ways can I snuff him in his sleep?"

And just when I thought this conversation would finally end (For the love of God, make him stop talking), he rambled on, clearly on a roll and oblivious to the expression on my face.

"And I love that we're both okay with that. Yep, even with that Parkinson's thing and all that shaking you do, you're still a beautiful woman..."

(wait for it)

"...especially for your age."

Our server, who was within ear shot, set our wine down with a wince and an "Ouch!" while Hubs sat beaming, wearing that proud grin men get when they present their wives with a "really cool" vacuum cleaner for their anniversary ("You're going to love this, sweetie! It's got 48 attachments!"), then are totally baffled when they don't get a drop-everything-you're-doing-because-it's-time-for-some-visible-gratitude-baby naked happy dance in return. My cheeks were cramping from trying to hold a smile, as I grit my teeth and mumbled "Thanks...I think."

We finished our wine, and Hubs was all smiles about our romantic evening, while my brain was spinning for ways to explain why comments like "even with Parkinson's" and "especially for your age" should never come into any conversation with your wife, regardless of the point you're trying to make. Unless, of course, you're good with no sex for the indeterminate future or, if she holds a grudge, quite possibly forever.

Then again, he did say I was beautiful, and I'm reasonably certain he intended his long-winded, unfortunate, although enthusiastic, monologue to be a compliment. I'll just go with that. But we're going to need more wine.

"Every time you find humor in a difficult situation, you win."

~Anonymous

They Get Boxers. We Get Spanx.
WTH??

Standing in my closet this morning, trying to decide what to wear, it occurred to me that this decision is often determined by what needs to go on *under* the outfit. Men have it easy. At whatever age they answer the cosmic Boxers vs. Briefs debate for themselves, they're good to go, like, *forever.*

We remain faced with a vast sea of daily options, from the ubiquitous thong (stupidest fashion design, *ever*. If you're thin, under 22, and have never given birth, you *might* pull this one off. For the rest of us, it's an all-day wedgie and looks like dental floss wrapped around the bottom of a Weeble), the French-cut brief (good choice, if you don't mind panty lines rippling diagonally across your backside like a geographical fault line), the full brief (the most flattering *under* your clothes, but in the laundry pile, look like Grandma Bertha's undies. I fold my own), or finally, Spanx.

In a dizzying variety of lengths and mission statements, these puppies can stuff your body into an otherwise out-of-the-question ensemble like a southern belle's corset. They take some time to master and can cause a Parkinson's patient to toss them through the nearest open window into the neighbor's arborvitae in a moment of uncontrolled frustration, but once you're in, you'll be strutting that 35th high school reunion dress like you *own* it.

As with all great ideas, however, Spanx are not without their design flaws.

For Spanx to work, they need to be *tight*. The whole point is that they make you look firmer and smaller than you really are. If you can slip them on like drugstore pantyhose, they can't do their job.

Having said that, there is, for unfathomable reasons, no pee snap.

Seriously?? HEY, SPANX PEOPLE! In the *entire* design process, not one of you obviously-male-and-will-never-have-to-actually-wear-one geniuses said, "So Dudes, I was looking at our designs this weekend, and does anyone else here wonder if we might have a logistics problem, given the basic concept here (shoehorning size X booty pop into size Y slip of slingshot fabric) if she *ever has to pee.* Maybe we should put in a snap"??

But, alas, not to be. My advice? Pee *before* you get dressed and go easy on the liquids for the rest of the day.

As I was getting dressed, it became depressingly clear that as the "bloom of youth" was gone forever and several previously sexy body parts had migrated south, defying all attempts to coax them back up into their original longitude. My undergarments had become less frivolous and more functional. Less about wisps of lace whispering "Hey, Sailor, new in town?" and more about lifting, stuffing, and otherwise coaxing recalcitrant areas into clothes I used to wear with ease.

And Parkinson's brings its own list of challenges to the Spanx table.

Simply put, if you struggled with Spanx before you got Parkinson's, you now need to add an extra 20 minutes to your morning routine. Reduced grip strength and balance issues can make these almost insurmountable if you're trying to put them on by yourself.

It helps a lot to have a Spanx buddy, preferably one that will help you get them on with minimal guffaws and witty, running commentary. Hubs would appear to be the obvious choice, since he's just down the hall and even my closest girlfriends are less than enthusiastic over having to stop by on their way to work to help get my not-inconsiderable backside into a spandex girdle roughly the size of my Chihuahua. But I hadn't yet reached the point where I was ready to have Hubs see me trussed up like a Thanksgiving turkey underneath my sexiest dress. He's very visual, and some things can't be unseen.

Finally selecting a dress and its most suitable Spanx counterpart, I decided to fly solo and get that new-age girdle on by myself or die trying. I spent the next 15 minutes wriggling, cramming, and yanking the tightly knit miracle worker into place. First, you yank it up on one side, alternating with a "hop-wiggle" to shimmy it into position, then repeat on the other side, alternating until you're saddled up and ready to ride.

But feel free to make this sequence your own. Most days, yank-wiggle-shimmy can simply be repeated until everything is properly placed. But there have been occasions when I got caught up in the rhythm, adding a little "boom" hip check between repetitions. Think cruise ship conga lines. Yank-hop-BOOM with one hip, the yank-hop-BOOM with the other. (Don't judge. Some days we're just making lemonade.)

Under any circumstances, this is easier to do if you're standing, but if you have balance issues, make sure you have something to grab onto if you start to topple over. The last time I tried to do this without a spotter, I ended up grabbing the air in a freefall, finally face-planting onto the floor, with my butt in the air and my Spanx twisted somewhere around my thighs, with nary a cover around my nether regions. Hubs came tearing down the hall to see what the thud was, and will now forever refer to what he walked in on as "not my best presentation."

But I persevered on my own (yank, hop, wiggle-shimmy on my left; yank, hop, wiggle-shimmy on my right; repeat) until, sweaty and triumphant, I was *in*.

Fifteen minutes later, as I was standing in the bathroom in my full-coverage, get-those-suckers-*up-there* bra, with thigh-length, waist-to-hips, bounce-a-quarter-off-your-ass Spanx model #916, Hubs walked in and promptly burst into boisterous laughter, choking out, "What the HELL are you *wearing*, woman?!?" Mortified, I punted and assumed a sultry expression, "Keep laughing, fella. You know you want me."

"That may be true," he chortled, "but how would I get *to* you??"

Getting old is not for the faint of heart.

"A good time to laugh is any time you can."

~Linda Ellerbee

EXCUSE ME IF I
DON'T SHAKE YOUR HAND.

Cleaning Your House?
Don't Forget Your Maid's Costume

Cruising a local used-book store, I stumbled across
Marabel Morgan's 1974 best-seller "The Total Woman." A quick
glance through the worn pages and the $1 price tag made it too
much fun to resist, so I took it home and settled in the outdoor
lounge chair for a read.

The Total Woman promises to "make your marriage come alive" by following Ms. Morgan's simple suggestions on how to keep your man in love with you.

(Some years after the book was published, Marabel got divorced. We can only assume that she snapped from the pressure of trying to keep a spotless house, raise perfect and *quiet* children, cook like a gourmet chef, and find her husband endlessly fascinating *at all times*, all while wearing a maid's costume for spontaneous sex in the dining room, until she ultimately threatened to stab her man through his ungrateful, selfish heart with her pearl-handled fondue fork. But hey, that's just my theory.)

Ms. Morgan claims that "since a woman cannot change her husband, she should accept him as he is and change herself." (Some things you just can't make up.) Apparently "it's only when a woman surrenders her life to her husband, reveres and worships him" (at this point, my two previous divorces were beginning to explain themselves), "and is *willing to serve him*, that she becomes really beautiful to him."

I'm so screwed.

For those of you who haven't read The Total Woman, but who are open to a few suggestions to revive your faltering marriages, here are a few of Marabel's more memorable tips:

1. Look beautiful and put together every morning when he leaves for work, so he wants to come home to you at the end of the day. Seriously??

I get up at 5 a.m. and start my day with foot stretches to limit the time it takes for the dystonia (such a pretty little word, until you figure out that any word that starts with "dys" doesn't usually end well) to resolve itself so I can get to the kitchen without having to hop on my good leg, while simultaneously shaking my cramping foot like a dog after a tree pee, trying to get the cramp to release so I can grab a Pop Tart and a Diet Coke because I can't take any pills on an empty stomach, let the dogs out to pee, unload the dishwasher, throw in a load of laundry, fold what's in the dryer, make the bed, shower and get ready for work in something other than yoga pants and a Walmart t-shirt. On days I need to wear makeup, add another 20 minutes. I skip this whenever possible. Hubs says he comes home because we're married and he's legally required to be here. I'm good with that.

2. Take an active interest in his hobbies and learn about them so you can talk about them, or even better, *participate*. Yeah, no. Hubs loves to fish, and (big surprise), he's *never once* asked me to go with him. Hubs fishes to get away from his worries, his work, and, let's be honest...me.

And, of course, there was that one unforgettable and unfortunate time he declared that "that shaking you do" would scare away the fish. Apparently I can make an entire boat vibrate. Go me. But ultimately, since he fishes to be alone, it would defeat his search for serene solitude if I hopped in the boat and asked, "Do you mind if I bring my cell phone?"

3. Greet him at the door every day in a new fantasy sexual outfit (oh, and have sex *every day* to keep the spark alive). I'm a writer, and the only response I can think of here is "ARE YOU HIGH??" Completely dismissing the admonition to have sex every day since that's a personal preference (and if you *are* doing it every day and you're in your 50s, good for you), her outfit of choice is "nothing but Saran Wrap and a bow." While I'm all for trying something new from time to time, Parkinson's makes it difficult to turn towards your backside, necessitating outside help to get properly swathed in see-through kitchen wrap. A quick mental review of family members or friends I'd call for this particular favor resulted in "Oh, hell no."

Besides, shrink-wrapping my baby belly and smashing down my boobs in clear plastic, then tying a big red bow around my neck and greeting him at the door all de-feathered, trussed up, and shaking like a seriously pissed off Christmas turkey seems a bit like the gift from hell.

I decided at this point that Hubs would just have to make do with our messy life and his imperfect wife. He came home one evening, and as I strolled down the hallway, fresh out of the shower and wearing nothing but the outfit the good Lord gave me, to ask about his day, I realized he wasn't alone. Oh. My. God. Hubs was laughing so hard he couldn't introduce his new friend, and I'm never coming out of the bathroom again. *Ever*.

Maybe I should've worn the Saran Wrap.

"Always laugh
when you can.
It's cheap medicine."

~Lord Byron

Hello?
Is Anybody Out There?

Hubs and I do a lot of entertaining. Our favorite way to spend an evening is with a couple of friends, some great wine, lots of good food, and laughing 'til our faces hurt. Hubs loves to host and is a master griller, never letting the unpredictable Pacific Northwest weather intimidate him into canceling his plans. He's been known to barbecue in the snow, and rain doesn't even slow him down.

One year, he built an umbrella attachment to the side of the house, directly over the bbq'er, and since then, drive-bys checking out the crazy man bbq'ing in a torrential downpour have introduced us to more neighbors than a 4th of July block party.

Recently Hubs came home from the store and I could tell by the multiple overstuffed grocery bags that we were expecting guests for dinner. He then announced that they were arriving in an hour. I dashed down the hall to begin what he calls "my process," while he started dinner preparations.

(13 years of marriage has finally convinced him that leaning against the bedroom doorway, sighing and repeating "How much longer?" like an annoying meditation chant is virtually guaranteed to double my metamorphosis time, and if he wanted any help at all, he'd stay clear of the bathroom until I came down the hall with table linens in my hands.)

About the time I was trying to figure out how to pull up my Spanx with one shaky arm, I thought I heard him shout out about "running somewhere to get something." But at that moment, I was singularly focused out how to stuff my body into a spandex toothpaste tube without breaking a menopausal sweat or toppling over into my shoe rack.

Spanx, while unparalleled in terms of cramming a size 10 butt into size 8 pants, were not designed for Parkinson's patients. Go buy a pair, hold them up, and the problem will immediately present itself. Simply put, they're smaller than the body part you're trying to cram into them and they require a bit of work to get them properly placed. It helps considerably if you have two smoothly functioning hands with good grip strength.

For those of us riding the Parkinson's bus, the only system that seems to work is to use our "good arm" (the one that doesn't shake) to yank up one side, add a little hop to settle the body part in, then reach over to yank on the other side, add the hop, and repeat, taking rest breaks as needed. Yank, hop, breathe.

Yank, hop, breathe. And for the love of God, pee first, or you'll be in the bathroom so long, the entire group will storm the gates to see if you're okay.

One evening event, it took just a little too long, and the concerned guests were banging on the door, ready to burst in and save me. I panicked and tore the shower curtain off the rod, frantically trying to wrap myself up before eight people became scarred for life busting in on a 57-year-old woman, naked from the waist down except for her Spanx bunched around her knees. It took an entire jar of Spackle to repair the wall damage, and we've never seen those people again.

As I finally settled into my lower-body Spanx and a ridiculously expensive push-them-up-to-where-God-originally-put-them magic bra, I smiled, visualizing Hubs's delighted surprise when he got home and found me all fluffed, smelling yummy, happily setting the table. The universe, however, had other plans.

As I slipped my dress over my head, somehow I got my tremor arm up in the neck hole, causing my head to get caught in an arm hole, and (please God, don't let this be happening), I was stuck. I'm talking *wedged in*, with one arm up in the air, waving around like a children's sock puppet, my head jammed in tight and completely covered...can't breathe, can't see... with my good arm pinned to my side. Can't pull it up. Can't pull it down.

Are you kidding me??

Did I mention that one of the more unique side effects of Parkinson's is what they call On/Off time? Every now and then, your body (and brain) just sort of "switches off" for a few seconds and you freeze up. It's like your brain saying, "You need to get out of bed" or in this case, "You need to pull this dress off," and your body replying, "I'm aware of our predicament. Give me a minute, buddy." The dress was stuck and my switch was off. Awesome.

Unable to perform the necessary sequence of actions that would extract me from fabric hell, I hopped blindly down the hall to my phone (smacking into the wall half a dozen times before finally toppling against the kitchen counter...yeah, that hurt), apparently thinking what? I could dial the touch pad with my toes?? Ultimately realizing that my only options were to a) tear the dress and rip it off (love this stupid dress, so yeah, no), or b) stand there, immobile and blind, one hand waving in the air, and wait until Hubs got home. Well, crap.

Days later (or 20 minutes, depending on which one of us is telling this story), he walked in the door.

"Fifty bucks if you DON'T ASK, DON'T LAUGH, and just GET ME OUT OF HERE!" I yelled, muffled through the fabric.

Most of the time, when Hubs finds me in these types of circumstances, he helps first, then dissolves into whatever level of amusement he feels appropriate for the situation at hand. Today, however, his immediate, boisterous merriment and the unmistakable "clicking" sound of my iPhone camera told me he wasn't taking the deal.

Next time, I'm wearing sweatpants. Elastic waistbands *understand* me.

"You grow up the day
you have your first real
laugh at yourself."

~Ethel Barrymore

SEXY IS SO OVERRATED.

I'm Bringing Sexy Back.
This May Take a Little Work

Hubs and I are big Netflix fans. It's an easy, commercial-free way for us to watch our favorite TV series together at any time we choose, so bedtime at 9:00 doesn't preempt watching our prime-time faves. While our movie tastes are diametrically opposed (he's all SyFy or political thriller, while I'm content to rerun *The Notebook* every evening until I die), our TV tastes are totally sync'd. *Prison Break, Boston Legal, Sons of Anarchy, Breaking Bad, Friday Night Lights.* (One particularly cold, snowy weekend, Hubs made a huge pot of chicken & dumplings and we marathoned 11 seasons of *Frasier* in three days. Gained four pounds and never got out of our jammies the entire weekend, but was it worth it? Oh, yeah.)

Great series selections aside, we don't actually *watch* most episodes. Hubs refers to it as shows we *talk* through. Thirteen years together and our favorite evening activity is to pour some wine, put in a DVD, and proceed to talk through the whole thing. (Needless to say, we've been banned from the local theater since 1993.)

One evening, while watching an episode of Smallville, I was firmly entrenched in the middle of a story I was telling, when I noticed Hubs staring at the TV with a slightly glazed expression and a goofy grin. Not used to being upstaged by the TV, I looked over to see what had him so enthralled. It was a shower scene, showing the silhouette of Lois Lane striking a sexy pose, with her back arched, head thrown back, and one toe pointed. Hmmm. Well, that doesn't look too hard. Not having seen that particular expression on Hubs's face for quite some time, I decided to give it a whirl during my next shower.

Later that night…

Hopped in the shower and called for Hubs to bring me a towel. Blithely ignoring any Parkinson's-related balance issues or spontaneous muscle cramping when trying something new, I waited until he entered the bathroom, at which point I arched my back, tossed back my head, and lifted my knee to show off a toe point worthy of Swan Lake.

What I learned in that instant was that a) I am not a Romanian gymnast, b) tossing my head back makes me dizzy, and c) if one has balance issues, one should not attempt to stand like a yard-art flamingo in the shower.

Before Hubs had time to be properly dazzled, my back went into wrenching spasm, promptly followed by screaming foot cramps and loss of balance, causing me to pitch forward, flailing unsuccessfully for something to grab onto, until I knocked out the shower door and tumbled out onto the floor, screaming "Owee! Owee! Owee!" while hanging over the edge of the tub, face planted on the tile and butt in the air.

By now, Hubs is doubled over *howling*, choking out, "What the HELL are you doing??" When I told him I was trying to look like Lois Lane in the shower, he dissolved into another fit of apparently uncontrollable merriment. "But she's 22!!" he chortled, "and you're..."

Wisely refraining from finishing that sentence, he got very busy replacing the shower door, trying (unsuccessfully) to stop looking over at me and bursting into laughter all over again. I got up and dried myself off with as much dignity as I could muster and, head held high, I went down the hall to put on his old sweats. They're yummy comfy and twice my size.

Apparently sexy is not my thing.

"A person who
knows how
to laugh at himself
will never cease
to be amused."

~Shirley MacLaine

A Glass of Wine, a Sippy Cup, and a Totally Unsponsored Post

Those of you who read my posts (or who just hang out with me after work) know that I love all things red and winey. And the redder, the better. None of that Pinot Noir nonsense. I'm a Cabernet girl at heart.

When I hold my wine glass up, I don't want to see silly sunshine filtering through the liquid. Give me some of that full-bodied, big-butt, oaky yumminess. It's my drink of choice, and I would never think to cheat on my beloved Cabs with Patron shooters or fruity martinis, no matter how cute the glasses are. I'm faithful to that which I love, so my little Cabernet grapes have no worries that I'll wander.

Which wouldn't be a problem if I weren't a klutz. And not in an adorable little "Oops, how did that shoe get there?" klutz. I'm talking a trip-over-there's-nothing-there-and-*there-never-was* klutz. And that was before Parkinson's. Give a klutz Parkinson's, and she'll spend more time on the floor than standing up.

When we bought our first house, Hubs announced a new rule that stated "No walking with wine glasses," trying unsuccessfully to decrease the number of times I would get up from the couch, full wine glass in hand, trip over yet another imaginary object, invariably upending an entire glass of dark red tannins down my shirt and onto the carpet.

The other problem is that I'm an animated speaker (big surprise). Botox notwithstanding, I have a lot of facial

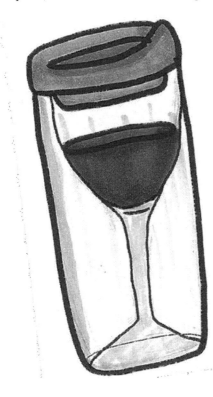

expressions, which are invariably accompanied by equal amounts of arm waving, and all that motion tends to send red wine sailing over the rim like mini tidal waves in a glass. We settled half that problem by eliminating all stemware, which tends to snap like a chicken bone during the telling of a truly great story (especially when knocked against a wall or banged onto a coffee table to emphasize a particularly entertaining point) and going to stemless wine glasses.

While they did cut down on broken glass in the vacuum cleaner, but weren't so much help in the spillage department.

Hubs consequently implemented Rule #2. All wine glasses, stemless or otherwise, must be held in the non-tremor hand only. Exaggerated, dramatic gestures, while holding a glass of wine with my tremor hand have been known to shoot a rather impressive arc of wine clear across the room.

Ironically, I also love white t-shirts. Specifically white t-shirts from the Gap, which I order in bulk. All that airborne wine has to go *somewhere*, and it invariably starts down the front of my favorite white t-shirt. And although I'm a virtual encyclopedia on how to get red wine stains out of carpets, the red wine vs. cotton battle still eludes me.

Shortly after Hubs and I were married, I was excitedly telling a *great* story, waving my arms for emphasis, at which point a healthy swell of wine sprayed up and over the edge of the glass, landing smack in the middle of my up-to-that-moment pristine white t-shirt, right between my breasts.

Hubs looked over and said, dryly, "Yeah, I married up."

It has been suggested by family and close friends that I either give up white clothes altogether or switch to white wine, to which I always reply, "White wine is for wussies. Where's the sport in *that*?"

Years ago, BH ("Before Hubs"), I was married in a traditional white wedding gown and my mother followed me around for the entire reception like a mama duck, poised to catch the glass at the end of every spontaneous, boisterous toast. Saved the dress, but Mom was exhausted and slept for two days. When Hubs and I got married, *he* wore white. *I* wore (big surprise) bright red bugle beads, strapless, form-fitting to the floor. I looked like I should have been lying across a baby grand piano singing "I Want to Be Loved by You." Hubs loved that dress (and Mom had a lot more fun at the wedding).

And now, 14 years later, I'm still in love. With Hubs, and with red wine.

We've had a great journey, and hopefully have many more years to come. In the meantime, I've recently discovered the coolest product ever for wine lovers (especially wine lovers with Parkinson's). It's essentially a clear acrylic, stemmed wine glass inserted into another clear acrylic tumbler, with a sippy hole. Where has this been??

So now I'm taking my new wine-filled, non-spillable, unbreakable sippy cup down to my computer to check out the Gap online store. I hear they're having a t-shirt sale.

Part 3

It Takes a Village

"Don't let what you can't do stop you from doing what you can do."

~John Wooden

Sweaty Cologne, Insane 25-Year-Olds, and a Trip to the ER
Fitness Can Be Brutal

There are certain advantages to the aging process. You're wiser, you're (hopefully) more patient and less judgmental, and your priorities are often less about how you look and what you drive, and more about who you are and what you have given back to the world.

And of course, there's grandkids. After the responsibility of raising your own children and ensuring that they're socially acceptable before their launch into society, grandchildren are the universe's way of letting you now spoil the crap out of a tiny human, then promptly hand the over-sugared, thoroughly entitled delight back to their parents for repair.

There are certain aspects of aging, however, that are not so thrilling.

Menopause (Really, God? *Really*??) weight struggles, gravitational body changes, and often, physical limitations due to unexpected medical diagnoses, all conspire to remind us that time is moving forward and since we no longer have the inherent fitness granted by simply being young and healthy, we're going to need to explore more direct approaches. In other words, we need to get off our middle-aged butts and get some exercise.

As I explored various options for getting back into shape, I mentally reviewed some previous attempts (occurring in earlier decades and pre- Parkinson's, so all fails then would be epic-level now).

Yoga. WTH? First of all, the dominatrix teaching the class is *not* your Zen friend. She's all "Reeeeach. Breeeeath. Stretch furrrrrther."

Well, hell, if I could do *that*, I wouldn't be taking your stupid class. And have you ever noticed that *none* of these poses are named after humans? Nope. Standing Tree. Downward Dog. Frog, Cobra, Lion, Camel, and Crocodile. Do you know why?? Because humans weren't built for these positions. They are *not natural*. Virtually every position they demonstrate starts with the premise, "You know the way your body *wants* to go? Go the *other* way."

A now ex-friend recommended something called "Hot Yoga." An hour later, I was upside down, my not-inconsiderable behind stuck in the air, while staring through my inverted legs at a total stranger's butt-crack, as Brut-scented sweat (seriously, dude?) rolled off his matted armpit hair and puddled into sticky pools two inches from my face. It used to take me at least three dates to get there with a guy. And he'd have bought me dinner first. Brut guy and I had *no* business sharing sweat pools at this stage of our relationship.

Some months later, at my son Jake's suggestion, I ordered a series of exercise DVDs called "Insanity." Guaranteed to get you "boot camp ready" in 90 fun-filled workouts. Completely disregarding the average age of the models on the cover (22) and the fact that I'm, well, *not* 22, I placed my order and anxiously awaited my 12 DVDs, plus Nutrition Guide and "Workout Success" wall chat to map out my ever-ripping muscles over the course of the next three months.

The first DVD was one of those annoying Preliminary Fitness Tests you take to see if you're fit enough to get fit. Uh, okay. 20 minutes in, I'm on the floor, red-faced and hyperventilating like a freaked-out Chihuahua in a thunderstorm, staring at a large, flashing red screen that essentially stated: "Do Not Continue This Program. You Will Die. Go Sit in the Corner, Have a Doughnut and a Diet Coke, then List This Kit on eBay. Remember to Include the Nutrition Guide You Obviously Never Intended to Read and the Ill-Named Success Chart. Maybe You Can Get Your Money Back." Middle age sucks.

Then I saw an ad for those sneakers with the little balance pods on the soles, guaranteed to improve your posture and tighten your glutes "while all you do is walk." Who could resist? One might think that after three decades in sales, I'd at least be a tad skeptical, if not downright snort-wine-out-of-your-nose-while-you-scoff cynical about hard things being made to look easy, and that's usually true. But claims of shortcuts to weight loss and firmer butts tend to make my left brain explode, while simultaneously making my right brain behave like a dog hearing, "Wanna go for a walk?" Tail starts wagging, body's twirling, and face says "Oh boy! Can we? Huh? Can we? Oh boy, oh boy, oh boy!"

Got home and happily laced them up, envisioning my soon-to-be military posture and peach pit butt from which you could bounce a quarter, when I noticed a small warning label on the box that read, "Do not wear while exercising." Huh? I promptly filed that under silly instructions like "Do not take while operating heavy machinery" and fired up a dance DVD. Having a ball until I grapevined into a side lunge, stumbled off the front pod, and took out my coffee table. Three stitches later, I hung up my shoes.

And so, after much searching, I finally settled on a newer, kinder DVD series (think Richard Simmons meets Jane Fonda: The Later Years) that alternates working recalcitrant upper and lower body parts each day with a series of floor exercises and cardio. There's lots of dancing and wiggling, which is a Parkinson's dream workout, since we pretty much wiggle all the time. And the class wasn't full of 20-something, already buffed, professional dancers. Their moves were as goofy as mine. Even my doctor would have been hard-pressed to single out who had Parkinson's and who didn't in this group. Besides, shimmying and shaking around my office in the wee hours of the morning is less intimidating and just more *fun* when the instructor and the music come from my generation ("My generation??" God, I just became my mother).

One morning, I was busting my best floor moves, feeling all stretchy and strong, when they got to lower body wall squats. *C'mon*, people. I couldn't do those in *high school*. Four decades later, with Parkinson's balance issues forever banning me from step ladders or stilettos, and the loss of left-side body strength, I'm thinking they didn't get easier.

Up against the wall, legs at 90 degrees (okay, 45. Don't judge), then hold it.

F-o-r-e-v-e-r. 10 seconds... 15... starting to tremble. 20... 25... I'm moaning by now. "Oooh, oooh, yi, yi, yi!" At 45 seconds, I shouted out, "Oh. My. *God!*"

Suddenly Hubs's voice booms out from the bedroom, "I don't know what the *hell* is going on in there, but you'd BETTER BE ALONE."

I laughed so hard, I toppled over and hit my head on the ironing board.

Tomorrow's another day. I'm thinking pancakes for breakfast.

"The question is not how
to survive,
but how to thrive with
passion, compassion,
humor, and style."

~Maya Angelou

But You Should See Me Parallel Park

I was in my thirties when my mother finally taught me how to parallel park. Pull up parallel to the car in front of the space you're aiming for, crank a hard right, look over your shoulder to "site in" your spot, then back up, counting 1001, 1002, immediately following with a hard crank to the left, then just slide in, snug as a bug. Works every time, virtually eliminating parking by Braille (bumper tap in front, back up a bit; bumper tap in back, scoot forward a tad), and impresses the hell out of the 20-something set, since they apparently don't bother with this in high school Driver's Ed classes anymore.

Parkinson's, by decreasing my flexibility, has put a small cramp in my ability to dazzle my offspring, particularly since this includes the often-necessary-especially-when-driving shoulder look-over. Obviously, parallel parking is much easier when you're looking in the same direction your car is moving. Parallel parking with Parkinson's is more of a "crank right, count 1001, 1002, crank left, pray, then back up blind and hope for the best."

Notwithstanding my belief in the power of prayer, this approach makes me extremely nervous, which, oddly enough, turns out to be a good thing.

My hand shakes in direct proportion to my stress level, dramatically increasing the effectiveness of my apology to the guy whose car bumper I just whammed into.

Seriously, who's going to yell at an anxious, middle-aged woman, repeating "I'm so sorry, I'm so sorry," while she shakes like a crack-addled hummingbird? (I know, shameless Parkinson's exploitation, but didn't you ever use your hot youth to get out of a speeding ticket? This is the senior version.) Virtually guaranteed to get Angry Guy apologizing to me for parking so close to the line. The last guy offered to buy me a drink until I calmed down. He was a darling young pup, but I figured it was a good time for me and my assault car to get out of his line of sight.

What I *can't* do, now or ever, is back up. Nada. Nyet. Nope. Not at all.

I couldn't do it before Parkinson's, and now even a mid-backup prayer can't help.

You know those side mirrors on your car that say "Objects may appear closer than they really are"? Evidently my brain sees things behind me and says "Objects are 45 degrees to the left. Go that way." This past year alone, backing out of my garage has resulted in the loss of four underground sprinkler heads, one small Japanese maple tree, countless garbage cans, the left corner of the petunia bed, and the previously long, fluffy tail on the neighbor's prized show cat (yeah, that one cost us).

And let's just toss into the mix that I tend to be what the DMV calls an "oblivious driver." When I set out to go somewhere, I'm more "horse to the barn" than "Oh, what a beautiful drive. Look at all the pretty trees, and there goes Aunt Freda. Hi, Aunt Freda!" When faced with a task, however big or small, my brain is permanently set on "Git 'er done," so I usually notice nothing in my way until we meet up close and personal.

And *Hubs knows this.*

But since I've never been one to dwell on my shortcomings, this morning I hopped into my little car, clutching my errand list in my left-sided tremor hand and iPhone in the right-sided steady one.

Parkinson's teaches you to sort carry items in direct proportion to the consequences of dropping them. Electronics, wine, and the family Chihuahua are safer and more secure on the right, where steady nerves and grip strength are still relatively intact, while nonessentials like To-Do lists and dry cleaning, being largely immune to being tossed around like wind socks on a blustery day, are fine on the left.

I was on my phone, getting directions to my destination, while I simultaneously backed out of the garage, still facing forward, trying to eject Hubs's AC/DC disc and find my favorite country station, steering with my knee to avoid sideswiping his Harley. All body parts appeared to be working as a team until I drove over the lawn, leaving two distinct tire marks on the wet grass, and finally reaching a full stop by plowing butt-first into a huge pile of bark dust in the driveway, showering red chips everywhere, just as Hubs pulled in.

Well, crap.

Hubs (waving his arms): *"I can't BELIEVE you reverse-plowed into that huge pile of bark dust!! SERIOUSLY?? How could you not have seen that?!?"*

Me: *"You piled it all in the DRIVEWAY, right behind my car! You know I can't look behind me!"*

Hubs: *"There were eight bags! EIGHT! I left you room to go around! I figured you'd at least LOOK at the driveway before you got into your car! "*

Me: *"HAVE WE MET??"*

Hubs (sighing): *"You're right. My mistake. I'm sorry."*

Me: *"You're forgiven. If you get a couple of rakes, I'll help you clean up your mess."*

Hubs: *"If I didn't love you…"*

Me: *"I know, sweetie. Trust me. I know."*

"Happiness is a decision."

~Michael J. Fox

I Still Got It.
I'm Just Not Sure What It Is

Aging in our culture can be tracked by a variety of achievements and obstacles. Graduating, college, marriage, babies, buying a house.

These are all milestones that provide a tangible record of the passage of time. Our *bodies* can also tell us that time has passed by swaying parts heading south and jiggling even when we're standing still, faces that show a life well lived (woman-speak for "lined like an old saddle in Texas"), and oftentimes, visible symptoms of conditions diagnosed during what is ironically referred to as our "golden years."

In our 20s, youth is the magic elixir that erases long nights of too much alcohol and too little sleep, sporadic exercise, and the stressors of new marriages, young children, and new careers. In our 30s, even if fit and fabulous, we're labeled cougars for eyeing young men in their 20s, while we're somewhat shocked to find out they think we're kind of, well, *old*.

During our 40s, young men call us MILFs (we could still be that boy's mama), and in our 60s, GILFs (our children now have children). But we look great and, surprisingly, are often more confident than ever, even with diseases that make us shimmy and shake like hip hop rap stars.

The 50s, however, are not as defined. At 50-something, you feel 30-something and, God or your plastic surgeon willing, you look 40-something. We'd like to think we're still hot, but body parts and faces are, damn it, starting to show *age*, and "hot" usually refers more to our body temperature, as we're hanging our heads out the car window like panting Labradors after two hours of Chase-the-Cat at doggie day camp.

And just in case you forgot for a blissful moment that you're not still the young prom queen of your graduating class, you get diagnosed with Parkinson's and your primary objective every morning is no longer how to diminish the lines around your eyes, but rather how to mask the constant, telltale motion of your arm by only buying clothes with pockets or remembering to sit on your hands.

This awareness of middle-age in a culture that worships youth (while not yet achieving the self-acceptance we often find in our later years) causes our vanity to occasionally whine for just a hint of reassurance that our best years are not in our rear view mirror and there will be more occasions to get out of our yoga pants, stuff ourselves into some Spanx, and show the world we've still got it.

Last night, Hubs and I were at our favorite local winery, and I was having a glass of wine (okay, three...don't judge), when

Hubs met up with another avid fisherman and they happily wandered off to compare "It was *this* big." "No way!" "Yes way!" fish stories, leaving me alone at the table, holding a lovely Cabernet with my good arm and sitting on the other.

A short time later, a friendly, nice-looking young man came over and struck up a conversation. Feeling flattered, I offered him a chair, and we talked for a half-hour or so about various topics, including his plans after college (OMG, he's still in *college*?), his family, the new car he wanted to buy (if he could get financing) and countries he wanted to visit someday.

I offered my thoughts and the occasional advice, until he finally gave me a long look and announced, with a big smile, "You know, I really liked talking to you."

I flashed my brightest "Bite me, middle age" smile, *until he wrapped it up with*, "You remind me so much of my mother. Her arm shakes like yours. Is that Parkinson's?"

"Uh, yes," I stammered.

"I thought so," he smiled, "She has it too. I haven't talked to her for a while, so if you'll excuse me, I'm going to go call her and see how she's doing."

My first thought was O*uch*! My second thought was Oh, what the hell.

Somewhere, an obviously much-loved young man is calling his mama, and apparently I had something to do with it.

I can live with that.

"Do not judge me
by my illness.
If you do, you'll miss
the amazing person I am."

~Anonymous

BIG HAND

LITTLE HAND

2 + 2 is...
Anybody Got a Calculator?

I was at the State Employment Office to take a series of skill tests that the State believed would help them match me to potential jobs. The 12-year-old test proctor seated me in front of a computer and sing-songed the instructions in an impressive one-take monologue. She took a second deep breath and nailed the explanation of the rules in one long sentence, wrapping it up with, "And for the love of God, turn off your cell phones, because I *don't* like to repeat myself." Good to know.

At the sound of a small bell, Baby Girl looked at her watch and recited "There are three areas of testing, seven possible levels, three questions each. No do-overs. You may begin."

#1. Reading Comprehension. Sailed through all seven levels. Perfect score. Piece of cake. (Seems I could have had that third glass of wine last night, after all.)

#2. Fact Finding. Questions #1-3. Done, done, and done. Ha. Maybe they'll let me leave early.

#3. Math. Oh, crap.

I've never been a "natural" about anything in the digit world. I don't know which came first, my unexplainable and persistent abhorrence of anything dealing with numbers in general, or if I'm just so *bad* at them, I've learned to simply avoid them at all costs. Now throw in a touch of Parkinson's and a new medication regimen, and the mountain just got higher.

New meds are almost always a struggle, bringing with them a host of new side effects. I was currently working through insomnia, alternating with extreme fatigue, complete loss of appetite for food or sex (sorry, Hubs), and six weeks of nausea reminiscent of the first trimester of pregnancy.

Bluntly put, *everything* made me want to hurl.

As those side effects slowly began to abate, a super-fun new one cropped up. A particularly frustrating and frequently embarrassing side effect that I call "Foggy Brain Syndrome." It's like your brain is under water and it takes you a half-a-beat longer to do even the simplest tasks or to recall a name of someone or something you've known all your life. In other words, you'll forever have a new respect for people with dementia, because that's *exactly* how these pills can make you feel.

And that's how Baby Girl learned that making assumptions (bad assumptions...*bad*) from my previous two scores might have been a skosh hasty. She fired up the computer, and with a few mouse clicks, boom, up popped "Math, Level Three." Before I could say, "Um, I have Foggy Brain Syndrome," she was off to another station.

So there I sat, medicated with anti-math pills and one arm shaking enough to vibrate my chair, causing the young woman next to me to lean over with a worried "Are we having an earthquake or something?" (By then my chair had vibrated six inches closer to her, making her question not altogether unwarranted.) Meanwhile, the other arm was frantically waving to get Baby Girl's attention so she could start me at a more realistic level. Too late. Baby Girl had left the room. So here goes:

Question 1: Percentages. I put the original decimal in the wrong place, causing a domino effect of incorrect preliminary answers. Awesome.

When I clicked "Submit Final Answer," my computer speaker immediately replied with a loud BONG! (Was that *truly* necessary?) to indicate *Wrong*.

Question 2: Tapped the screen, and it lit up with one of those annoying story problems about trains traveling in opposite directions and what time do they meet in Denver? I couldn't do those in high school, and supon hearing yet another loud BONG! (Again, *really* people??) when I submitted my answer, it was obvious that in the 40 years since my last SAT, my math skills remained as elusive as ever. At this point, I figured it couldn't get any worse, so I wrote on the worksheet "Don't know. Who cares? And who takes a train these days? Like, *anybody*??" Baby Girl was not amused.

Question 3: Fractions. Hate those little suckers. If you *meant* "half," *say* "half." "I'd like 5/10 of that candy bar" is just stupid.

By now, Baby Girl was collecting the worksheets, and as she leaned over my shoulder, she whispered, "Oh my." Looking at me in wonder and what could reasonably be interpreted as a little pity, she continued, "It appears we need to start you at Level 1. Okay sweetie?"

Then it got worse.

Level 1, Question 1: "Looking at the clock on your screen, if the little hand is on 4 and the big hand is on 10," (wait for it) "what time is it?"

Seriously??? I was laughing so hard, I almost fell out of my chair, and Baby Girl was staring at me like she'd just bitten down on something not quite right. It was definitely time for me to go. It didn't matter what the other questions were going to be. It was *math*.

During the Walk of Shame out to my car, I noticed a job opening on the bulletin board for a new librarian at the local middle school. I'm thinking of applying. When it's time for class, they just ring a really loud bell. I won't even need to wear a watch.

"A sense of humor is needed armor. Joy in one's heart and some laughter on one's lips is a sign that one has a pretty good grasp of life."

~Hugh Sidey

Today I Became a Boy Scout Merit Badge

When Hubs and I decided to sell our house of nine years, we were embracing the current boomer trend of downsizing, going from a charming, but high-maintenance little house that we loved, to a smaller, less time-consuming place that would free us up to get out and do something (anything) other than work in the yard or tackle yet another home renovation project from a seemingly endless list.

(Hubs pointed out that a huge percentage of those projects wouldn't have existed if I hadn't decided to periodically rearrange the furniture, move wall pictures around, or attempt any level of home repair, all of which invariably resulted in a steady stream of less-than-successful outcomes that became new weekend projects for him, and that since I would be moving *with* him to the new house, he was tempted to call this a "lateral move." Funny guy, my Hubs.)

Anyway, we ultimately decided to *really* reduce our monthly home-owning obligations for a year or two and just rent until we found The House that was worth a 30-year mortgage commitment. We quickly found a cute, clean, inexpensive rental in a great location, so we promptly plunked down 1st and last, packed up the Chihuahuas, and moved in.

The big question became what to do with our stuff. Furniture and belongings that once filled a house, a garage, *and* an attic were never going to fit in the rental. Hubs was adamant that he didn't want to have to re-buy all our worldly goods six months down the road if we found The House, so we packed it all up and put it in storage until we reached a decision in the ongoing renting vs. owning debate.

Three months later, we were two peas in a little snowpod and loving the rental life. One morning, Hubs announced, "I think we should have a garage sale. Let's sell all that stuff we've got in storage." Since I've never been a big believer in paying to store crap we're obviously not using, I agreed and we headed out to the barn to inventory our stash for the big day.

We spent the next several hours cataloging and pricing a dizzying variety of junk we once went into debt at 29 percent to buy, now selling for 10 cents on the dollar (and millennium kids wonder why our generation is broke).

Treadmill/coat rack? Used once. Gone. Mismatched plate set? Always drove me nuts. To-go pile. Enough Christmas decorations to righteously do up the White House? Kids are grown, and we now spend Christmas at the beach.

In the pile. A variety of appliances that don't work? Since Hubs is neither a mechanic nor an electrician, buh-bye. Souvenir wine glasses from our Washington wineries tour? The boomer version of collectible State spoons.

Nope. Skis/boots/poles? Haven't skied since before we bought the house we just sold. Why the hell do we still have these?? Old bedding sets from the last four times I changed colors in all the bedrooms? Even Goodwill won't take bedding. Five bucks says they're yours.

The final six boxes were the hardback books from a large bookcase wall in our previous living room. In these days of Nooks and Kindles, we decided to simply donate the books to the local library rather than haggling over the 50 cents we may or may not get for each individual book all day long.

Until Parkinson's, I was always the strong one in my family. For years, I was the one that opened new or stuck jar lids, carried in the heaviest bag of groceries, and pulled up the stubborn weeds with 5-inch roots.

Parkinson's, however, had pretty much obliterated my left-arm strength, making it unpredictable at best, and sometimes simply nonexistent. And then there's the balance issues that had resulted in more than one public and embarrassing faceplant when I wasn't paying attention or didn't see the obstacle in front of me. Together, these made carrying six heavy boxes down two flights of steep, linoleum-covered stairs arguably the stupidest idea I had all day.

I pulled up in front of the library and headed for the Customer Service desk, preparing to ask for help, preferably without playing the Parkinson's card. "Hello, I have Parkinson's" invariably makes the next several minutes somewhat awkward, as the person you're talking to begins visibly struggling for a politically correct reply.

At that moment, a charming young man with a beautiful smile opened the door for me and reached to take the first box out of my hands. "Wait here, pretty lady" he instructed, "and I'll help you take these downstairs."

Being a total sucker for flattery (however cheesy), I smiled back, feeling all young and girly, shoving my tremor hand into my coat pocket, out of sight. I watched as he bounded over to my car to get the remaining boxes, which he easily carried downstairs to the Donation Department. After six trips, he ran back up, and with a grin and an arm flourish, proceeded to take my arm and *help me down the stairs*.

As I was processing what was clearly the mortifying equivalent of a Boy Scout helping an old lady across the street, he then assured my therapist at least one more session with, "You know, my grandmother has Parkinson's, too. She fell down some stairs once and it took her a long time to heal, so you need to be careful."

Your grandmother? How old is your mother, you wet-behind-the-ears little puppy? Like, 30? Admittedly, the linoleum stairs were oddly steep, but YOUR GRANDMOTHER?

I waited until we got to the last step and had an "accidental" stumble, accidentally giving Baby Boy a swift kick in the shins. That was for his grandma. The elbow to his stomach? That was for me.

Grandma's still got it.

"A day without laughter
is a day wasted."

~Charlie Chaplin

Self-Service?
Isn't That an Oxymoron?

Having been in retail for, okay, ever, I have an admittedly high bar for customer service expectations. I know, I shop at Walmart, which creates untold emotional stress because I can't legally reach over and smack those people. (Whenever my son and I would go to Walmart and he'd see me start to hyperventilate, he'd calmly say, "Those people aren't paid enough to deal with you, Mom. Ask to speak to the manager.")

When I run into an obviously misplaced misanthrope in a customer service position, I tend to fire up fairly quickly. This propensity has not always worked out well.

I was out running errands, and I pulled into a gas station to wait for the gas guy. I waited...and waited...STILL WAITING...until I finally got pissy enough to charge into the mini mart to ask the three 20-something employees if any one of them might consider taking an actual *work break* out of their "And, dude, we were, like, *so drunk*" story swap fest to come and help me??

Two of them burst out laughing, while the 3rd rolled his eyes and smirked, "Lady, this is Washington. You gas it up yourself." *Seriously*, guys? How do I do that??

All eyes turned to Billy, the youngest party legend, who resigned himself, with a dramatic sigh, to somehow being cosmically chosen to help an exasperated middle-age woman, who seemed to have some sort of condition Baby Billy couldn't identify, but that made one of her arms shake like somebody stuck a quarter in it. Baby Billy wasn't taking any chances that I might be warming up to give him a good smackdown with that arm, so he slid off his stool and I headed back to my car, my reluctant gas Zen master in tow.

Billy showed me how and where to swipe my card, key in the amount I wanted to spend, and start the pump. My little car is a 1974, before the advent of gas tank levers inside the car. I've explained to every gas guy in town that there is no lever to "pop open." You have to do it manually, which requires a reasonably intact grip strength. Parkinson's loves to mess with that. (My blow-dryer has been plugged in for two years because I can't pull the plug out of the wall and I'm too stubborn to ask Hubs for help.)

But in spite of the shaking (which Baby Billy was trying desperately not to stare at) and my reduced grip strength, I finally managed to open the gas cover and stick the hose in. Feeling all Norma Ray "I can *do this*," I hopped back into my car, while we made small talk, waiting for $75 worth of gas to be funneled in. By now Baby Billy was getting positively chatty and a few minutes later, he handed me back my credit card and smiled, "There you go! That wasn't so hard, was it?"

Assuming "There you go" was gas-guy-speak for "You're done" I flashed young Billy my most dazzling MILF-Y smile and took off, with the hose *still in my car*. As I pulled away, it was ripped out of my car and began slamming repeatedly onto the pavement, spraying arcs of gas in *every* direction with each bounce.

Baby Billy is yelling, "HEY LADY!! STOP! STOP!" while the other two attendants are stumbling out of the mini mart, doubled over in laughter.

I wish I could say I did the right thing and stopped. I would be lying. I drove out of there like a bat out of the hell I'm obviously going to. In the meantime, I'm only shopping in states where I don't have to get out of my car.

"Laughter and tears are both responses to frustration and exhaustion.
I prefer to laugh, since there is less cleaning up to do afterward."

~Kurt Vonnegut

CALL ME WHEN THEY'RE GONE.

If You Need Me, I'll Be in the Bathroom.
With the Wine

I should have known the day was going south when we woke up to rain. Hubs and I were hosting our first "all-family" get together and had been asking God all week for sun so we could keep everyone outside.

But the Big Guy was apparently working on more pressing issues, because it was *definitely* raining. And like the sign you see in elevators, "Warning: Maximum 10 people," our dining room comfortably sat 8, and we had 18 coming over. Awesome.

As we tried to recall how exactly it came to pass that we were hosting this particular gathering, all we could remember was a recent barbecue with the sibs, where the conversation turned to holiday dinners at Mom and Dad's, and how Mom had single-handedly (Dads didn't start helping until the '90s) whipped out Thanksgiving, Christmas, Easter, July 4th, *and* all birthday/graduation celebrations for five decades. As she graciously served up feast after feast, year after year, she would assure us that, other than possibly setting the table, she "didn't need our help." We happily obliged and stayed out of her way, scarfing down veggie trays and chip baskets like we hadn't eaten in weeks, while simultaneously wiping out their bar. She should've smacked us.

And so it was decided that *this* year, we'd give Mom a break and have the next gathering at our house. How hard could it be?

The first arguments began over the menu. Most wanted ham. A few wanted turkey. One sibling thought we should go casual with burgers and potato salad. And of course, there's always *one* vegan in the group that thinks holidays would be a swell time for everyone to give up meat. It quickly began to feel like herding wet cats and, after a ream of flying texts and emails, we decided to choose our own damn menu. If you don't like it, bring a sack lunch. Moving on.

Off to the store, where we quickly discovered that feeding 18 people was *not cheap*. We decided to buy the ham, and scrambled home to start calling siblings with potluck assignments. (Yes, sibs, we *know* you never had to bring anything to Mom and Dad's, but we are *not* your parents, and we don't need to pay for your employed, adult butts to sit around our house and eat all day. You don't contribute, you don't eat.)

We spent two days prior to the weekend scrubbing the house with a toothbrush like it somehow *mattered* (It didn't), and now it was time to figure out where everyone was going to sit. Our dining table seats eight, max. Frantic phone calls to in-laws for card tables and folding chairs, and one trip to Wal-Mart for spare stools to seat kids at the kitchen island, and breeeathe... This could work.

Then God laughed.

As we looked out the window at the now-torrential downpour, cars began to pull into the driveway. The first sib, who was assigned mashed potatoes, showed up with a BAG OF POTATOES and asked "Where's a pot?" (For future reference, when I ask you to bring mashed potatoes for 18 people, I'm assuming they'll be *ready to eat.*)

The next group through the door included five grandchildren, all under the age of 10. Since Hubs and I don't have small children living with us, our house is decidedly *not* baby proof. Running from room to room, quickly putting all things sparkly and dangerous up out of harm's way, I missed the next influx, which included another sib, his wife *and* their friends from out of town that they "knew we'd just *love*." That's okay. I can eat standing up.

By now I was starting to hyperventilate and my Parkinson's symptoms were in high gear. Hubs refers to my tremor as my "Park-o-Meter," which he uses to identify exactly how stressed I am at any given moment. At that moment, I was shaking like a Chihuahua during a fireworks display, still blissfully unaware that the older kids were happily instructing the younger ones how to use the master bed as a bouncy castle, demonstrating that if you jumped real high, you could almost hit your head on the ceiling. The wailing screams of an unidentified little one who actually achieved said goal sent me racing down the hall to distract them by setting up a plastic bowling toy set down our hardwood hallway, but apparently it was much more fun to bowl towards the dining room, laughing hysterically as the adults repeatedly tripped over the little pins.

The last sib finally showed, carrying the remaining grandchild and a sack of rolls (Rolls? Really??), so we began to gather everyone to the tables.

Before we could say "Thanks for coming," a wee one knocked over a glass of chocolate milk and started sobbing, which got the baby screaming, so I picked her up and she promptly threw up down the entire front of my shirt. (And by the way, who the *hell* fed this baby Cheetos??)

In a final perfect moment, Hubs went to take his beautifully basted ham out of the oven, and it seemed the oven had somehow gotten turned off an hour earlier. SERIOUSLY?? As orders were shouted out for a pizza run ("Pepperoni, thin crust!" "The kids will only eat cheese!" "Vegan, dude, and double 'shrooms!"), I grabbed a bottle of red wine from our wine rack and quietly slipped into the master bathroom, locking the door.

My stress level was blowing up my Park-o-Meter, and I thought a little solitude and a glass (okay, a bottle...it was a *holiday*, people) of Cabernet would dial it down and keep me from inadvertently whacking somebody with my out-of-control tremor arm.

A few minutes later, I heard Hubs knock softly, "Are you in there?" "Yes," I sniffled, "My arm is shaking, and I'm not coming out until everybody's gone."

"That's okay," he said, "but open the door just a crack." I did, and his hand came around the door, holding a corkscrew and a box of Milk Duds.

Dinner is served.

"Remember me with smiles
and laughter,
for that is how I will
remember you.
If you can only
remember me with tears,
then don't remember me at all."

~Laura Ingalls Wilder

A (Wildly Premature) Letter to My Granddaughter

This weekend, I went to my uber-beautiful baby granddaughter's 1st birthday party, and as I was marveling at the changes that had occurred in her during the last 12 months, I began to visualize her life unfolding over the next several years. Playdates, preschool, first grade, ballet lessons, summer camps, boys…

Say what??

As I stared at this chubby bundle of darling on my lap, I realized that someday she will bring home a B-O-Y. (Parent speak for "OMG.") My mind immediately began formulating a list of things I wanted to tell her about young love and, you know...*boys*. Doing what writers do, I scrambled to write it down, and now, tucked away in a box for the future, is her "Letter to My Granddaughter."

Dear Kami,

I'm writing this letter after attending your 1st birthday party, where I realized that you will not stay a baby forever and that someday (*too soon*) you'll venture out from the happy, supervised world of Play-Doh and piano lessons to the uncharted waters of young relationships. Having lived through those years (before cell phones and, yes, electricity), and then raising your dad, there is much I want to tell that I hope will make this exciting and uncertain time a little less bumpy.

Rather than waiting until you're old enough to ask questions, I'm giving you this advice now, while I can still find my keys. And my house. (I'm counting on a long and happy life, watching you grow up, but Parkinson's can be a funny foe.) Grandmas can often offer more *practical* thoughts on subjects like dating, since your dad's solution will likely be to send you to school every day with well-trained military escorts, and your mom will use weekend grounding as a punishment for any and all transgressions, effectively keeping you in your bedroom, alone, every weekend between your 14th and 18th birthdays. Just remember, sweetie, they love you too.

1. If a boy tells you that he's "not good enough for you," believe him. Ditto if he tells you he's "not into a relationship right now." Translated: This means he's a loser and he knows it, and he's also dating your best friend. Move on.

2. Don't expect him to change, even for you. If he's a "player" (our generation called them liars and cheaters), a teenage alcoholic, or a bully, he'll still be one with you. Yes, people can change. Most don't.

3. Girlfriends are as important as boyfriends. At your high school reunion, you'll be more excited about seeing your girlfriends than your ex-boyfriends, whose names (trust me) you won't even remember. So think carefully before dumping a best friend over a boy. It's rarely worth it.

4. You can tell a lot about a boy by the way he treats his mother. Get over to his house for a dinner or two, and watch carefully.

5. Don't confuse the wedding with the marriage. We call this the "Kim Kardashian" syndrome (Google this). Little girls often dream of becoming brides, and the whirlwind of dresses, cakes, and flowers can be hard to resist, but the wedding lasts a day, while the marriage is, hopefully, forever. The question isn't "Do I want to marry this man?" It's "Do I want to spend the rest of my life with this man?" *Not the same question.*

6. Talk is cheap. If you want to know how he really feels about you, go deaf. Don't listen to what he *says* he feels. Watch what he *does*. Then decide if he's worthy of all your fabulousness.

7. Don't make decisions out of fear. Fear of not hanging out with the cool kids. Fear of never falling in love again. Fear of being alone. This jerk you're afraid to let go of? Ten years from now, he'll be living in a trailer with the missus, raising six kids and fighting over custody of the wiener dog. You come from a

long line of independent, strong females. He's good to you or he's gone. Period.

8. He should make you feel good, but it's not his job to make you *happy*. Happy is *your* responsibility. Develop a talent. Follow a dream. Find a hobby. Go to church. Volunteer. Go to college. Color your hair. *Laugh*. Be happy, with or without him.

9. Have somebody to talk to. Your mom and dad will always listen, but I know that's hard. Every generation thinks they invented true love, and believe it or not, I didn't tell my parents everything either. Girlfriends are okay, but they don't usually know any more than you do. Find a teacher, a counselor, or come on over to my house. My door is always open, and you can't say anything that will shock me or make me love you less. Ever.

10. Listen to your inner voice. If a flutter in your stomach tells you something isn't quite right about this guy or he's asking you to do things you don't want to do (have sex, drink, drive the getaway car), *run*, don't walk, to the nearest exit. If he persists, tell Baby Boy your grandma has a customized 3901 Beretta shotgun. And Parkinson's. I may hit one of his tires, or I may hit all four. That's what we grownups call a "crap shoot."

My aim may be questionable, but I can still pull the trigger. Maybe he'll get lucky. Maybe not.

Many experts say that we should not tell a child she (or he) is the most beautiful, smartest, amazing kid on the planet, because if said child finds out that's not true, she'll suffer lifelong trust issues as a result of having been lied to by her parents. Those people are idiots. You are absolutely the most beautiful, smartest, and yes, amazing girl in the world, and you deserve to be treated accordingly.

And if all else fails, bring Baby Boy to Grandma for a look-see. She loves you. And she's packin'.

Love always, my beautiful Kami,

Grandma

"The strongest people are not those who show strength in front of us, but those who win battles we know nothing about."

~Anonymous

MOMMY, WHY IS THAT LADY'S HAND SHAKING?

13 Things NOT to Say to a Parkinson's Patient

Sitting at our favorite restaurant, a girlfriend and I were happily sharing an embarrassingly large plate of nachos while we toasted everything that came to mind with our second round of margaritas, when a middle-aged woman came up to our table and said, with a bright smile, "Excuse me. I don't mean to be rude," (immediately clarifying that she was about to be) "but do you have Parkinson's?"

Pardon me??

As I sat there in frozen silence, mentally tallying the staggering number of social and political boundaries she just exploded through, I finally nodded and choked out, "Yes, I do. Thank you for asking."

"I thought so," she went on, "I was describing Parkinson's to my friend over there at our table, when I saw your arm shaking, and I told her that's what it looked like. Anyway," she chirped, as she walked away "You have a nice day, okay?"

Oh. My. God.

GF and I looked at each other for a long moment then burst into mutually unrestrained laughter. (What else could we do??) Thus began our conversation on the funny, the odd, and the downright bizarre responses I've had from people when they discovered I have Parkinson's.

Apparently the mere mention of a chronic illness makes everything their mothers ever taught them about social correctness simply vaporize and they blurt out the first thing that comes to mind. An hour later, we were snorting margaritas out of our noses from the often-unintended hilariousness of human nature (okay, and from our third round), and GF suggested I write a post about it.

"People obviously need help," she grinned.

While I realize it can be awkward during a casual conversation to suddenly find out the other person has a chronic disease, and it's difficult to instinctively know the "right thing" to say, there are certain things that are virtually guaranteed to offend.

So to help ease the difficulty of "What do I say now?" (and to reduce the possibility of a Parkinson's tremor arm shooting out and smacking you up 'long side the head) when a grenade suddenly gets dropped into your conversation, I thought I'd offer up some of the worst comments I've personally experienced over the last five years. As my mother always said, "50% of knowing what TO do is knowing what NOT to do."

13 Things NOT to Say to a Parkinson's Patient:

1. "Why are you shaking?" Unless you are five years old, this is just rude. It's like little Susie staring up at a large woman in the supermarket checkout line and asking, loudly, "Why are you so fat?" Hopefully, little Susie's mama will jump on this opportunity to explain to her tiny peach pit that one does not ask a total stranger about a visible physical condition. And if you can't ask at five, you can't ask at 50.

2. "Do you have Parkinson's?" If you don't know, we're not close enough for you to be asking that question. And what if I *don't* have Parkinson's? It's a pretty ballsy question if you don't know for sure. It's the same reason we don't ask a woman when she's due if we're not *really* sure she's pregnant. Some things can't be unsaid.

3. "Can you make it stop?" Assuming that you're referring to the tremors, uh...no. If I could, I would. Many Parkinson's patients endure nasty side effects of expensive medications for years, simply trying to reduce the tremor symptoms. If "just relax" worked, we'd be packing the ashrams and be the Zenningest group on the planet.

4. "There's no cure, right?" No, and thank you for reminding me.

5. "I heard you had Parkinson's." The problem with chronic illness is that it tends to override everything else you've ever accomplished. Now I'm visualizing that whenever my name comes up, every sentence ends with a whispered, *"And she has Parkinson's."* Awesome.

6. "What does your husband think?" WTH? I always want to answer this one with, "Well, he thinks he got hosed and insists that 'in sickness and in health' was rhetorical. I just remind him that I own half of his fishing boat and if he leaves, it stay."

7. "My grandfather had Parkinson's and was in a wheelchair until he died last year." Thanks for sharing that. But Gramps was 92 years old. And Parkinson's does not kill you. He didn't die from Parkinson's. He died *with* Parkinson's. And as for the wheelchair, I don't need one at this time, but if I ever do, you'll be the first person I call. Yeah, no.

8. "I read that people with Parkinson's only live another 20 years." Statistically, that's true. But most Parkinson's diagnoses occur in people over 60, so they likely only had another 20 or so years remaining anyway. But it's always nice to be reminded I've only got 13 years left.

9. "My husband's sister's Great-Aunt Flo had Parkinson's, but she started drinking goji juice every day and she stopped shaking." While it's always a pleasure to hear about someone whose Parkinson's symptoms were eliminated by eating kale or drinking berry juice, if there was a cure for Parkinson's at Safeway, Great-Aunt Flo wouldn't be the only person who knew about it.

10. "You should quit drinking Diet Coke. That's probably why you got Parkinson's." Choosing to overlook the rather sweeping judgment in *that* statement, unless you graduated from Johns Hopkins and specialized in Parkinson's disease, just be my friend, not my doctor, okay? Now put out your cigarette and let's go to lunch.

11. "It will all work out." What does that even *mean*? It's dismissive and cliché.

12. "God never gives us more than we can handle." So you're saying that God made me strong, and then just for giggles he gave me Parkinson's because he "knew I could handle it"? What the hell church do you go to?? With that reasoning, a loving God would have made me weak and cowardly. Then I'd have a life of rainbows and unicorns, where nothing bad ever happened to me because I'm not strong enough to handle it.

That's just stupid.

13. "Everything happens for a reason." A second cousin to #12, apparently referring to some cosmic governing body that needed me to have an incurable disease to fulfill some mysterious destiny, which I may or may not understand in this lifetime. I'm just supposed to "trust that there's a reason." What am I, like, three?? I'm 57 years old. Either tell me what's going on, or take this Parkinson's back. Also stupid.

"Okay. But what *do* I say?" you ask. A simple, but genuine, "I'm sorry" is always correct. We will direct the conversation from there. Some days, we want to talk about it. Other days, not so much. But thank you for caring.

Now, what's new with *you*?

"Tracy's big challenge is not having a Parkinson's patient for a husband. It's having me for a husband. I happen to be a Parkinson's patient."

~Michael J. Fox

Hubs Speaks Out
"We Have Parkinson's"

Over the past several years, as society endeavors to include men in journeys previously traveled alone by women, we've been introduced to paternity leaves, male menopause, metrosexuals, and "mannys" that help parent our young offspring while we're out in search of world peace (or trying to drum up this month's rent before two parents, one manny, and a couple of toddlers end up living out of a two-seater convertible).

One expression being casually tossed around, invariably by the male in the relationship, is "We're pregnant." Seriously, dude?? Did you gain 68 pounds in the last six months? Do you hurl whatever breakfast you managed to gag down earlier at the mere mention of raw meat?

Are you going to eject a 9-pound human out of a 10-centimeter orifice while she repeatedly tells you to 'just breathe through it'? No? Then *you* are not pregnant.

But on a recent trip with a couple of our best friends, I distinctly heard Hubs say, "We have Parkinson's." WTH?? Before I could reach over and smack him with my tremor hand, he continued. "She may be the one diagnosed, but it's changed my life too, and nobody ever asks about that." He was right. Five years after my diagnosis, we'd never talked about how it has affected *him*. Up until now, it had always been about my battles. Apparently he had his own, and was prepared to share.

He turned to face our friends, choosing to be "interviewed," as he called it, by neutral parties, while I sat quietly in the corner with a Diet Coke and a doughnut, promising to let him speak without interrupting, overreacting, or getting all butt-hurt by something he said. So here goes.

Hubs' list of "13 Ways My Wife's Parkinson's Has Changed My Life."

1. I used to leave my phone in my truck, checking messages once or twice during the day. Now it's attached to me like a toddler harness at Disneyland. If she calls, she might be locked in the bathroom, or she's impaled herself with a fork, or she's offering up a pole dance (in which case, I can be home in 10).

2. My wife is fiercely independent and a bit of a control freak. Parkinson's has forced her to lean on other people. I've learned to help her when she finally asks, without a running

commentary on why she didn't call sooner or how the hell this happened in the first place.

3. I no longer have any expectations of what I'm going to walk into at the end of the day when I get home. Kitchen fires, her stuck in a dress because she put her head through the wrong hole, or chasing the neighbor's cat through our living room. I'm flexible.

4. We love to dance and do a fairly enthusiastic swing. I've learned not to let go of her, though, after she twirled out the open front door one time and landed on the front deck before I realized she wasn't coming back.

5. I research the side effects of her medications so I know what to expect. If you don't know that tiny pill will make her as nocturnal as an alley cat, eating Lucky Charms at 3:30 in the morning because she can't sleep, or hallucinating and pointing out people at the foot of your bed who aren't actually there, you might start thinking she's just snapped and now you're married to a crazy person with Parkinson's.

6. Laughter is our strongest connection. Whether she's frustrated, sad, or just pissed off at this disease, my job is to help her find the funny. If I have to hop down the hall on one foot, shaking the other one like a cat trying to dislodge dog poop off its paw, in a goofy imitation of her working through her morning foot cramps, then that's what I'll do.

7. I've learned not to say "We already talked about this yesterday," or "Geez, don't you remember??" when she brings home a movie we just watched last week or needs me to repeat an entire conversation we had the night before. Constant reminders are annoying, sort of a Parkinson's equivalent of "Are

we there yet?" being repeatedly sing-songed by a back seat full of four-year-olds.

8. Her safety is an ongoing priority. We sold her Vespa because her tremor made it unstable. This year we did the same with her shotgun. As entertaining as it was to watch her wave the gun around, hitting whatever got in her path, the old guys at the shooting range were running out of places to hide when it was her turn to shoot.

9. I've learned that any compliment that includes "for Parkinson's" is not going to get the response I hoped for. "You look beautiful, even with Parkinson's" got me rocket-launched into the guest bedroom one night, and I've never made that mistake again.

10. I can gauge her moods with almost 100% accuracy by her tremors. I call it her "Park-o-Meter." Whether she's anxious, angry, tired, or sad, she has a certain tremor for each mood. Poker players call it a "tell." She has a warp-10 tremor that can only be handled by wine and Milk Duds, so my job is to have a stash on hand at all times.

11. I can't leave for work in the mornings until I know what she's wearing and if she needs help putting it on. Anything requiring something called "Spanx" is not as much fun as it sounds and is a two-person job.

12. We've always taken turns getting big-ticket items we each want. One year I bought a Harley. The next year, she redecorated the house. I haven't taken my turn since 2010. I look at her, especially when her symptoms are in high gear, and my heart breaks, so I give her my turn. This year, however, I'm

getting a fishing boat. I'm probably going to hell for being a bad husband, but I'm getting a boat. (He grinned.) Really, I am.

13. I've learned not to anticipate what the future will hold. Parkinson's is different for everybody. But this didn't just happen to her. It happened to *us*. If I could wave a magic wand and make it go away, of course I would.

Hopefully, they'll find a cure. But soon enough for her? Maybe, maybe not. Our other option is to find the funny and laugh about it. If I can do that, I'm giving her the best I've got to give. And that's a wrap."

Now, if you all will excuse me, I think I need to go hug my husband.

"Be strong. You never know who you are inspiring."

~Anonymous

The 20 Best Things About Having Parkinson's

I grew up with five siblings. Three older brothers and two sisters. Needless to say, we were like a veritable pre-school, with at least one kid being sick pretty much most of the time. All the childhood diseases came and went through our house, along with colds, allergies, flus, and whatever other non-life-threatening virus was running unabridged down the hallways of our local schools, shared freely and enthusiastically amongst the student body. I never got any of them.

I was always the "strong one," who never got sick. I'm talking *ever*. So over the years, I began to believe in my own omnipotence against disease.

Sickness was for weak people. For people who *wanted* to be sick. Since I didn't want to be sick, I wouldn't ever get sick.

Then, five years ago, I was diagnosed with Parkinson's. How was this possible?? I never asked to be sick. It's not like I listed it on my letter to Santa. (Dear Mr. Claus, I said "PONY," not "Parkinson's." Fire that idiot elf and get somebody who speaks *English*.) But yet, here it was.

Parkinson's is what they call a "designer disease," (Well, at least I like *that* part. Yes, I'm shallow. Don't judge), meaning everybody manifests symptoms a little differently and progresses at different rates. One of the most common symptoms, however, is a visible one-sided tremor, usually of the arm or hand, which I had. In spades. Well, crap.

As years went by, however, my innate love of situational comedy took over, and I discovered that the tremor, while inconvenient and sometimes embarrassing, had its uses. Simply put, we Parkinson's patients rock (bad pun intended) certain tasks. What the hell, if you've got to have a disease, particularly one with no current cure, you may as well learn to get it working for you.

On that note, here's my personal 20 Ways Parkinson's Tremors Come in Handy.

1. Rocking your fussy grandchild to sleep. Give Mom and Dad a break. Five minutes with us, and the little wailer is *out*.

2. Freaking out a burglar. Who needs ADT? Put up a yard sign that says "The Owner of This House Has a Shotgun. And Parkinson's. Good Luck." Sleep well.

3. Fertilizing the yard. We can sprinkle *acres* without tiring. Give us the fertilizer bag, and we'll see you at lunch.

4. Blow-drying our hair. Hairdressers say blow-dryers cause less damage if you move them quickly from side to side, as opposed to holding them steady. 'Nuf said.

5. Cooking and baking. We can whisk eggs. All. Day. Long. And you need sprinkles on those cookies? Just hand over the jar and walk away. We got this.

6. Feed your fish. Need a little shake of food twice a day? One good tremor twitch and the Goldie twins have got *exactly* the right amount of dinner.

7. Sex. Since this is a family-friendly site, that's all I'm going to say. The rest is up to your imagination. (C'mon, it doesn't take *that* much thought.)

8. Pet the cat. We can do this for *hours* without tiring. Seriously, our arms are moving anyway. You may as well stick a cat under there.

9. Applying makeup. Makeup artists say that blending is more important than application. We just hold up the brush and let the tremor do the work. Perfection.

10. Tossing tinsel on the Christmas tree. Everybody loves those little silver strands, but nobody likes having to place them onto the tree. Hand those individual strands to your closest Parkinson's relative. She'll tremor-toss them as long as it takes, until that tree glows in the dark. Merry Christmas.

11. Channel surfing. But I got to warn you. We're fast. You may need to be an Evelyn Wood speed reading graduate to keep up, but give us a remote and we'll show you how it's *done*.

12. Craft projects. See "Cooking and baking." Only with glitter.

13. The perfect martini. If you like them shaken, not stirred, we're your dream bartender. We can host any size party with ease. And if your blender goes blades up? A little extra enthusiasm (okay, a swig from the martini shaker), and we can offer up one fabulous margarita.

14. 52 Card Pick-Up. Got restless kids in the house? Give us a deck of cards. We can shoot those things in 10 different directions, 3 rooms away. It'll take the little hummers hours to find them all. You're welcome.

15. The shimmy dance. Admittedly more goofy than sexy, but we can spontaneously bust this move while doing almost anything else. Sometimes a little hard to turn *off*, but virtually guaranteed to get even nasty old Aunt Betty laughing.

16. Campfires. And I'm not talking about the EZ, light-in-a-pit things using presto logs. I'm talking "Survivor" fires, with no matches. The ones where somebody has to rub two sticks together, really, really fast, until they combust. Hand over the sticks. We'll call you when dinner's ready.

17. Dusting or cleaning. We can wipe, dust, or clean any surface in your house faster than a team of Molly Maids. Show us a dirty spot, then stand back and watch the blur.

18. Sewing. You want a crooked line cut in that fabric? We're human pinking shears. Not so good on the straight stretches, but for non-fraying hemlines? We're golden.

19. Wedding toasts. Oh, please. Piece of cake (Bahahahaha. I crack myself up). Find us a butter knife and a champagne glass, and we can quiet a room faster than the guests finding out the best man just drove off with the bride's mother.

20. Make popcorn. None of that wimpy microwave crap either. The good stuff, that requires tedious moments of pan shaking standing next to the stovetop. Oh, you want a bowl for a late-night movie? No problem. Just get us out of bed, prop us up next to the stove, and put our sleep tremors to work. Yeah, we're *that* good.

So the next time you're faced with a task from above, ask a shaking friend.

We can help. And we won't charge extra for the Parkinson's.

"I'm happy that I have brought laughter, because I have been shown by many the value of it, in so many lives, in so many ways."

~Lucille Ball

Lessons I've Learned from Parkinson's

In 1957, Steve Allen, a popular TV personality, was credited with the oft-repeated writer's quote, "Time plus tragedy equals comedy." Michael J. Fox referred to this quote in a recent interview, and added (paraphrasing here) that he preferred to go directly from tragedy to comedy, without the undue waiting in between. Michael, I like your style.

I've never been much for standing around, waiting for the grapes to ferment before I enjoy a glass of wine. My brain seems permanently set on "Chop, chop, people. Let's do this!" When I was officially diagnosed with Parkinson's, I spent a brief period working though the shell-shock (primarily letting go of the last shred of denial possibility), then launched a search to find the funny.

If I was going to live with this for the next 20-30 years, I was decidedly *not* going to spend it trudging through the five stages of grief. Denial was over. Anger was a waste. Bargaining seemed fruitless (I already had the disease). Depression was so...well, *sad*. Acceptance was an option if it didn't involve giving up, but even that sounded too passive. For me, laughter was the only suitable response to what was coming.

Five-plus years later, I had a manuscript pile of real-life anecdotes, stories, and musings on the lighter side of Parkinson's. I've also learned some powerful lessons about living with a chronic illness.

1. It can happen to you. No one is immune from illness. You say you've never been sick? You do all the "right things"? You've never smoked, you eat kale and drink acai juice every day, and you only use organic cleaning products? Good for you, but don't be smug. Sometimes it just happens.

2. You may never know why. True of many chronic illnesses, but particularly with Parkinson's. Since medical science has yet determined the actual cause, you will probably never actually know *why* you got it. "Why me??" is the Great Unanswerable Question. Let it go.

3. Don't lay everything at the feet of Parkinson's. One day I miscalculated a step and toppled off of a stepstool. Hubs freaked and promptly banned me from any and all ladders. I reminded him that I was a klutz who fell off ladders *before* Parkinson's, and will continue to do so probably forever. Every stumble isn't necessarily a sign of Parkinson's progression. Sometimes, it's just a stumble.

4. If you find you can't do something you used to enjoy, find a way to modify it or find something else. Yes, if you have a tremor, there will be things you either can't do as well or possibly shouldn't do at all. But if you can do what you love without needing to be good at it (playing the piano), then do it anyway. If it requires an ability you no longer have (target practice with a shotgun), find another hobby. Who knows? You might discover a new passion.

5. Don't look back. Endless wailing about "what used to be" is self-pitying and guaranteed to send friends and family scurrying in the opposite direction after the first 12 hours.

6. Give it so much attention and energy, then stop. You need to be aware of what you can and cannot do, and stay on top of your medications, but other than that, go live your life. You are not Parkinson's. You *have* Parkinson's. There's a difference.

7. Stay off the Internet. For the love of God, stay off the Internet. Nothing will make you want to bungee jump without a rope faster than an hour on WebMD, looking up every horrific, worst-case scenario of your illness. If you want to educate yourself about Parkinson's, talk to your doctor or get information from recognized Parkinson's research foundations.

8. The world will not stop. When potentially devastating events happen in our lives, we somehow expect that the world will stop and take notice. It won't. People will go on about their lives no matter what's happening to you. Don't take it personally. Before you were diagnosed, you did it, too.

9. You have to be your strongest advocate. *No one* will care as much as you do. If your medications aren't working or you don't like the side effects, ask your doctor for a different prescription. If you don't understand something, ask questions. And keep asking until you do understand. If a new symptom scares you, get in to your doctor, even if it's "not time yet." This is not the time in your life to let other people drive the bus.

10. People will treat you differently. Chronic illness makes people uncomfortable. They often don't know what to say, and it can remind them of their own vulnerability (see #1). Again, don't take this personally.

11. "What ifs" are exhausting and completely unproductive. Stop it.

12. You are not to blame. You didn't cause this by drinking Diet Coke or not eating kale. Don't heap self-blame onto the laundry pile of emotions you'll experience. The fact is, no one knows what causes Parkinson's.

13. Your life will change. The good news is that Parkinson's won't kill you. The bad news is that you'll be stuck with it for 20+ years, so you better learn to live with it. For me, it's about finding and sharing the funny. Other people get involved in fund-raising and awareness efforts. Whatever gets you out of bed and living a joyful life is a good thing.

14. It's okay to be angry or sad. But it's not okay to stay that way. *Everyone* has days where we shout "SERIOUSLY??" to the cosmos, or spend the day in our footie pajamas, eating Ben &

Jerry's Chunky Monkey ice cream by the quart while watching the entire series of *Little House on the Prairie*. But a day is different than a *life*. When my sibs and I were young and had bad days, Mom would tell us, "You get 24 hours, then you're done." Still some of the best advice she ever gave us.

15. Even without a cure in your lifetime, you can fight a good fight. There will be countless frustrations, epic fails, and a wealth of embarrassing stories to delight your offspring around the dinner table. If you can laugh, you will own that moment. And ultimately, a life made up of joyful moments means you've won.

More Praise

"I laughed, I cried, and I laughed some more. This lady takes Parkinson's and kicks its butt with care, dignity, and a wallop of humor. Inspirational and a must-read for anyone who wants to know about Parkinson's, or who just wants to laugh."

~Piper George, Blogger, *Talk About Cheesecake*

"Vikki has a special talent for making you laugh and cry at the same time! She can put her wonderfully humorous spin on a typically sensitive subject like Parkinson's and leave you in tears on multiple levels, and you will love her for it!"

~Angela McKeown, Blogger, *Momopolize*

"You know you've found a wonderful writer when you discover their work and you MUST ignore all your plans for the rest of the day, just so you can read everything of theirs you can find. This is exactly what happened when we first read Vikki Claflin's writing. Whether she's talking about aging, marriage, or life with Parkinson's, you know she will have you laughing out loud and wanting to call your best friend and tell her about it too. She uses humor to make everything so relatable that you find yourself nodding along the whole time you're reading. Trust us, once you read Vikki, you'll be hooked and won't want to miss a single, hilarious word!"

~Lisa and Ashley, aka "The Dose Girls,"
Bloggers, *The Dose of Reality*

"**Vikki has an eye for the absurd,** and she's not afraid to use it. Her writing cuts straight to the point – and the point always makes me laugh."

~Karen Irving, MSW
Managing Editor and Social Media Advisor, *Smarter Shift*

"**Vikki Claflin is the face** of middle-aging gracefully (and sometimes not so gracefully)! Her hilarious blog, Laugh Lines, offers up snort-inducing takes on everything from underarm waddle and muffin top to accidentally answering her son's Skype call naked and trying to lose the same 10 pounds since 1974. From hot yoga to hot flashes, you'll laugh your way to the conclusion of every story, as you thank God you're not alone out there. Now Vikki is lending her signature humor to her struggle with Parkinson's. With courageous wit, she tackles her most personal issue yet. You'll be inspired!"

~Parri Sontag, Blogger, *Her Royal Thighness*

"**Vikki Claflin is responsible** for incontinence in four out of five readers, from laughing at her writing! Her ability to laugh at herself and her way of making any situation funny is simply amazing. I am proud to call her a friend and fellow blogger!"

~Sarah Almond, Blogger, *The Sadder But Wiser Girl*

"**Vikki is one of the wittiest** people I know. Her writing is punctuated with humor and spirit and always makes me smile."

~Mindy Trotta, Editor, *Better After 50*

"**Have you ever laughed so hard** that you've been thankful you weren't drinking your morning coffee at the same time? THAT'S the kind of writing you get when you check in on Vikki. Her smile alone is contagious, but her words? Uplifting and fun!"

~Andrea Bates, Blogger, *Good Girl Gone Redneck*

"**Intelligent. Witty. Funny**. Those three words sum up how I'd describe Vikki and her writing. From marriage to everyday life, I often find myself laughing and relating to what she has written. Her posts about her marriage are downright hilarious and are things any married couple can understand. I consider her a must-read, if you want a good laugh."

~Kim Ulmanis, writer, *Kim Ulmanis*

"**Vikki Claflin brings a giggle of delight** and a smile of recognition each time I read her work. She finds humor in the most mundane of ordinary experiences, particularly the rollicking (not really) time of midlife. This funny lady lets nothing go unskewered. If I ever need a pick-me-up, I pick up Vikki's writing."

~Helene Cohen Bludham, Blogger, *Books is Wonderful*

"**Vikki Claflin is a wonderful writer,** who can make you laugh with the simplest story. She also excels at writing about the serious. She just does it in such a way that you find yourself smiling and laughing as you read about living with chronic illness."

~Tracie Nall, Blogger, *From Tracie*

"**They say laughter is contagious**. That has never been truer than in Vikki Claflin's case. You can't help but catch some when reading her blogs. She never fails to put a smile on my face with her humor, which flows not only from her funny bone, but from her heart, touching on topics we can all relate to."

~Janie Emaus, Blogger, *Janie Emaus*

"**Vikki Claflin can make me laugh through anything**. She is hilarious, but also warm, compassionate, and smart. A good doctor would prescribe her writing as a sure cure for whatever ails you."

~Lois Alter Mark, Blogger, *Midlife at the Oasis*

"**When a blog post from Vikki comes** to my inbox, a smile immediately spreads across my face. I know that no matter the subject, Vikki delivers sidesplitting laughter every time. Her writing is pure delight!"

~Linda Wolff, Blogger, *Carpool Goddess*

About Vikki

Vikki Claflin lives in Hood River. Vikki is an international best-selling author, humor blogger on laugh-lines.net, and an inspirational public speaker. She lives in Hood River, Oregon, where she writes the award-winning humor blog *Laugh Lines: Humorous Thoughts and Advice on How to Live Young When You're... well...Not*, where she doles out irreverent advice on marriage, offers humorous how-to lists galore, and shares her most embarrassing midlife moments.

Vikki has been featured on the Michael J. Fox Foundation website, Erma Bombeck's Writer's Workshop, *The Huffington Post, Scary Mommy, Midlife Boulevard, Better After 50,* and *Funny Times Magazine.* She also received a BlogHer14 "Voices of the Year" Humor award.

Shake, Rattle & Roll With It: Living & Laughing with Parkinson's is Vikki's first book. She has also written *Who Left the Cork Out of My Lunch? Middle Age, Modern Marriage & Other Complications,* available on Amazon and everywhere books are sold. Her next humor anthology, *Chin Hairs and Back Fat: Somewhere Between Tweezers, Yoga Pants & a Box of Wine* is coming soon. In the meantime, you can find more of Vikki's writing at http://laugh-lines.net.

Here's a Sneak Peek at

~~~~~~

Who Left the Cork Out of My Lunch?

By
Vikki Claflin

"At once frank and funny, edgy and heartfelt, *Who Left the Cork Out of My Lunch?* is a laugh-out-loud romp through midlife. Every woman over 40 should buy this book, and buy another for a girlfriend. Vikki Claflin is us. Pour a glass of wine, put on your Depends, and settle in with this hilarious read. Aging may suck, but Claflin makes it suck just a little less."

~Jenna McCarthy, Author
I've Still Got It…I Just Can't Remember Where I Put It:
Awkwardly True Tales from the Far Side of Forty

~~~~~~

Big Girl Panties Society. Rules for Membership

The first time I heard someone say "Put on your big girl panties and deal with it," I burst out laughing and spit my wine across my computer keyboard. My mind had an instant visual of a middle-aged woman sword fighting in nothing but her underwear. My brain goes places others' don't.

I decided then and there to start up a "Big Girl Panties Society," created to celebrate midlife women warriors.

We've been through our 20s, when anything was possible. We wanted it all, and we wanted it all at the same time. And we believed we could have it.

Through our 30s, we were focused on career climbing, finding potential soul mates, raising future world leaders, and struggling to make mortgage payments for houses we couldn't afford.

By 40, we began to come to terms with who we were and what drove us or made us happy. And we began weeding out what didn't. Many of us were on our second marriages and bearing the battle scars of divorce.

Now we're 50-something and a bit like the Velveteen Rabbit. He's a little worn, an ear lopped off, a button or two missing, and seams no longer straight, but a better bunny for his journey. We're independent, irreverent, opinionated, and fiercely loyal to those we love. We diet if we choose to, but cheat with no apologies. Exercise activities are selected as much for their fun factor as for their ability to give us firm thighs. We've discovered that spoiling our grandchildren is easier than raising our kids.

We've traded stupid stilettos for fabulous flats, and we're still hot. Sex is better than ever because we've learned what we want and we ask for it. We're happiest when we're surrounded by friends, sharing a great bottle of wine and laughing 'til our faces hurt.

If you're a woman warrior, you're in. But like any club, there are a few rules for membership.

1. **You should have experienced some level of menopause.** This gives you street cred when the group conversation inevitably turns to how to deal with night sweats and fatigue. We lose patience with 30-year-old Beach Barbies claiming they'll never take drugs for menopause symptoms because it's a *natural* process. It makes us want to smack you and make notes to remind your future estrogen-popping self what a bad-ass you were at 30.

2. **You should have a rudimentary knowledge of music from the 70s-80s.** At least enough to know that Kanye didn't "discover" Paul McCartney. How else will you be able to join our nostalgic, wine-induced, group karaoke during girls' night out?

3. **We request that all cell phones be turned off or put on vibrate** during group meetings. This includes luncheons, spa days, wine tastings, book club gatherings, in-home retail parties, and shopping excursions. This is *our* time.

4. **You must not use the word "like" more than once in any single sentence.**

5. **No comments or quips shall be made about the group's 10 p.m. curfew.** If you want to stay and boogie-oogie-oogie (and

you should know what that means) until last call, slip quietly into the women's bathroom until we've all gone home.

6. **You must be a grandma, be pushing your offspring to make you a grandma, or at least have a grandma in your immediate peer group.** This helps us establish that you share the same historical time frame as the rest of the group. And if your boobs haven't yet fallen off their perch and migrated to your waistline, you have an unfair advantage when it comes time for our coveted, annual summer "Best Boob-Belt" award.

7. **You cannot be offended by swearing.** We've earned it.

8. **At any group gathering that involves food, there will be no mention of weight, calories, or diets.** We're 60. We get to eat.

9. **There must be at least one current fashion trend in your closet that you're wearing the second time around.**

10. **You should be able to recognize at least two elevator songs as those you dated to in your 20s.** Extra points are given if you have the original songs on your iPod.

11. **You must be willing to view dozens of photos of grandchildren,** while listening to lengthy, detailed examples proving unequivocally that the tiny tot is obviously gifted (he can already count to 3!). Requests within the group for references on little Henry's pre-application into John's Hopkins, Class of 2032, must be honored.

12. **You must agree to share names and contact information,** if asked, about where you got that gorgeous handbag, who cuts your hair, or who does your Botox.

13. **No whining**. The purpose of our group is to provide support and encouragement to each other. While we're always willing to lend a shoulder and some advice (if you ask), your repeated, prolonged wailing about circumstances you have no intentions of changing will be respectfully removed from the agenda.

14. **What is said among the group, stays in the group**. We're not in high school. Tattling or rumor-spreading about any other member will get your ass summarily booted out the door.

15. **You must be able to laugh at yourself**. Various body parts have shifted downward like underground fault lines. Hair has stopped growing on our heads, but is now sprouting on our chins. Thighs jiggle when we're standing still. We gain weight on two Cheerios and a Diet Coke. We wear "age-appropriate" clothing. We have to record any show we want to watch that comes on after 10 p.m. We love sex, but we're usually too tired to have it. If you don't see anything funny about this, we're probably not the group for you.

I suspect that there are lots of women warriors out there. Let's find each other and celebrate. We're *fabulous*.

Also From Mill Park Press

Magic Fishing Panties by **Kimberly J. Dalferes** (Humor): A book that reminds all women of certain truths: the best pals are gal pals; all anyone needs to rule the world is a pair of black boots and a fabulous red coat; and above all else, live out loud, laugh often, and "occasionally" drink tequila.

Who Stole My Spandex? Life in the Hot Flash Lane by **Marcia Kester Doyle** (Humor—Marriage & Family): A witty selection of stories from Doyle's madcap world of menopausal pitfalls, wardrobe malfunctions, and a family full of pranksters. No topic—no matter how crazy or unimaginable—is too taboo.

Midlife Cabernet: Life, Love, & Laughter After Fifty by **Elaine Ambrose (Humor):** Here's proof that there is life, love, and laughter after fifty. Won the Silver Medal for Humor from the Independent Publisher Book Awards and a 4-star review from ForeWord, and ranked #1 in humor sales on Amazon. *Publishers Weekly* reviewed the book as "laugh-out-loud funny!"

Made in the USA
Middletown, DE
15 August 2018